HOW TO WRITE & ILLUSTRATE CHILDREN'S BOOKS

AND GET THEM PUBLISHED!

HOW TO WRITE & ILLUSTRATE CHILDREN'S BOOKS

AND GET THEM PUBLISHED!

CONSULTANT EDITORS

TRELD PELKEY BICKNELL

AND FELICITY TROTMAN

NORTH LIGHT BOOKS

Cincinnati, Ohio

A QUARTO BOOK

Copyright © 1988 Quarto Publishing plc

First published in the U.S.A. by
North Light Books an imprint of F & W Publications Inc.
1507 Dana Avenue
Cincinnati, Ohio 45207

ISBN 0 89134 264 8

This book was designed and produced by
Quarto Publishing plc
The Old Brewery, 6 Blundell Street
London N7 9BH

SENIOR EDITOR Kate Kirby

EDITOR Lydia Darbyshire

DESIGNER Bill Mason

ILLUSTRATORS Norman Bancroft Hunt, Lorraine Harrison, Rodney
Sutton
PICTURE RESEARCHER Carina Dvorak

ART DIRECTOR Moira Clinch
EDITORIAL DIRECTOR Carolyn King

Typeset by Keyboard Graphics, London, QV Typesetting Ltd
Manufactured in Hong Kong by Regent Publishing Services Ltd
Printed in Hong Kong by South Sea Int'l Press Ltd.

Special thanks to David Andrews, Jack Buchanan, Mick Hill,
Pauline Rosenthal, Ross, Henrietta Wilkinson

CONTENTS

The Authors

CELIA BERRIDGE trained initially as a teacher, and subsequently studied graphic design at Central School of Art, London, where she now teaches part-time.

Since 1975 she has illustrated over 50 children's books, including five written by herself, one of which – *Runaway Danny* (Andre Deutsch) – was a runner-up for the Francis Williams Award.

Her other interests include research into children's perception of pictures, and a study of children's drawing, from which she produced an educational film, *Drawing Matters*.

She still makes frequent visits to schools, children's book groups, preschool play groups and teachers' centers to talk to children and adults about illustration or child art.

MARY HOFFMAN is the writer of over 30 published titles for children, from picture books to the full-length novel, both fiction and non-fiction. Since 1982 she has been a member of the panel of The Other Award, which commends progressive children's literature which breaks new ground in social issues. Mary Hoffman is an educational consultant to various UK TV programs and publishers, as a specialist in children learning to read. She spends about one day a week in schools, working with children, in London.

VICKI LEE'S work as an editorial assistant at William Heinemann in the mid-1970s inspired her to train as a teacher in order to share the wealth of published material she saw was available to children. After several years' teaching in primary education, she began training teachers focusing on children's literature and non-fiction material. She has co-written non-fiction books and acted as consultant to publishing houses, advising on text style and layout for non-fiction publications.

Born in Australia where she tried many things before settling into librarianship, BEVERLEY MATHIAS has worked in Australia, New Zealand and England. She first heard storytelling as a child at home and at church ceilidhs, and some of those stories are still part of her repertoire. Beverley has told stories to children in schools, public libraries, parks and shopping centers, on television in New Zealand and at the National Theatre in London. She uses traditional Australian tales as well as funny stories, poetry and music. She has compiled *The Hippo Book of Funny Verse* for Hippo Books and with Jill Bennett compiled *Pudmuddle – Jump In* for Methuen. Currently she is the Director of the National Library for the Handicapped Child where she is continuing to tell stories to children whenever possible.

GABRIELLE MAUNDER has worked across the entire range of education from kindergarten classes to master's degrees and is presently responsible for postgraduate and undergraduate courses in Language and Literacy in Education at the University of Surrey.

The two master's courses she teaches each have a component on children's books and reading, as does the Advanced Diploma in Language in the Primary School, a course of which she is Director.

Reviewer for *The School Librarian* and *British Book News*; consultant to the Open University for their Children, Language and Literature course, Gabrielle Maunder has tutored to the American Summer School on Literature for Children and edited a children's anthology published by OUP.

American TRELD PELKEY BICKNELL trained in fine art and English literature in New York. She has worked in publishing in Boston and London – as Art Editor at Houghton Mifflin; Art Director at Abelard Schuman, Longman Young Books, Puffin/Kestrel; and Consultant Editor/Art Director at Piccolo Books. She is now Creative Director and co-owner of Belitha Press, a packager and publisher. She has written 18 children's books in her own name and pseudonym and for several years taught at St Martin's School of Art and Camberwell School of Arts and Crafts, London.

CATHERINE STORR cannot remember a time when she did not want to become a writer. After numerous false starts, she at last had a full-length children's book accepted in 1938. It was published in 1940 only to become one of many wartime casualties, sinking immediately without trace.

By this time she had decided that she must have some other way of earning a living, and was studying medicine. After qualifying and marrying, she turned again to writing for her two daughters. The stories of *Clever Polly and the Wolf Again* were written for her second daughter, and what is probably her best book, *Marianne and Mark*, for the elder. Since then she has published six adult novels and over 30 books for children.

FELICITY TROTMAN was born in Belfast, Northern Ireland and studied graphic design at Canterbury College of Art. After a successful career in publishing, including a period at Puffin Books as fiction editor, and at Macmillan Children's Books as fiction and picture book editor, she has spent the last five years freelancing for the BBC, Hamish Hamilton and Methuen Children's Books among others.

Her publications include *The Sorcerer's Apprentice*, *Marco Polo* and (together with Shirley Greenway) *Davy Crockett* in *Great Tales from Long Ago* (all published by Methuen) and *The Easter Book* (Hippo).

DOROTHY WOOD started in publishing as editorial assitant at Allen & Unwin (now Unwin Hyman) with the late and legendary Sir Stanley Unwin. From there she came to the US where she became associate editor at Pantheon Books, and spent some time traveling the country, working at whatever job came along.

On her return to the UK she started work for Kaye Webb at Puffin on a temporary basis, and stayed nine years. She edited the Picture Puffin list, produced the children's magazine *Puffin Post* for two years, edited Puffin non-fiction, and Peacocks. In 1978 she joined Scholastic Publications as Editorial Director to start a paperback list (Hippo Books) for whom she still works.

Introduction

The Art of the Storyteller

Storytelling has for centuries been a way of passing on the traditions and beliefs of a society from one generation to the next – both as written texts and as oral tales told by traveling poets or by a talented village storyteller. Their modern counterparts are today's authors. Often they are gregarious people who enjoy sharing their creative talent more directly than through the printed word. Some authors welcome the opportunity to tell their stories to a live audience. Authors writing for children have been known to tell and retell, carefully to change, refine and revise a story prior to publication as a result of telling it to audiences of children. This oral method of sharing words and story between author/teller and audience can be an important influence on the growth and development of a new writer.

THE ORAL TRADITION

The oral tradition of storytelling is one of the oldest art forms still in existence. It is a form of literary communication practiced all over the world.

An Egyptian papyrus known as the "Westcar Papyrus" appears to include the first known description of storytelling, although early Greek writing also refers to the telling of stories without actually detailing where and why it was done. Greek and Roman writers are responsible for the term "bard" becoming part of the English language. It was used to describe someone who related events or told stories. There is a record of a bard in Wales as early as 1200. As in Ireland, Welsh bards came to have a precise place in their society and a role to fulfill within the community, a role which is still important today. The early Norse used the term *thulr*, which means poet, for the reciters of long heroic poems such as

Beowulf. In Russia, minstrels sang *byliny,* or oral poems, and groups of entertainers known as *skomorockh* traveled around the country singing, dancing and telling tales.

Indian storytellers wandered from village to village carrying a large picture cloth called a *kalamkari,* which they spread out and used to illustrate the story they were telling. In China, traveling poets visited the homes of the wealthy, entertaining their guests with stories, while in Japan, the most famous storytellers were the Ainu women from the north.

The storyteller tradition in Africa is rich. The peoples of the Congo, the Xhosa of southern Africa and the Swahili all have within their culture long story poems which were recited by several storytellers in each village. These epic poems, called *griot*, are still recited in West Africa by hereditary bards – the skill

The storyteller still plays a central role in the rich cultivated life of African tribesmen.

and status passing on from generation to generation. Equally, the nomadic tribes of North America and the Aborigines of Australia have an immensely rich oral tradition with stories, songs, poems, religious and tribal customs – the whole of a complex culture – carried down through the centuries by the spoken word.

Storytelling has always been a means of passing on traditions and codes of behavior and of maintaining social harmony. Through his or her skill, the storyteller can convey religious beliefs, "explain" the mysteries of the natural world, reinforce the codes of behavior of a particular community, or transport the listener into an inner world of fantasy.

When stories came to be written down – and later printed in ever-larger quantities – their power remained undiminished and the storyteller, whether speaking directly to a small group or reaching millions through radio, television and the printed word, is as important to a largely literate world as he or she was to a largely illiterate one.

WHY TELL STORIES

- To help children learn to listen.
- To enlarge the listener's vocabulary.
- To extend a child's knowledge of the worlds of fact and fantasy.
- To stimulate the listener's imagination.
- To create an appetite for words.
- To introduce the shared activity of storytelling – from author or teller to audience.
  Storytellers are the direct medium between the story and the audience, able to change pace, alter or explain a difficult point, dramatize or play down an event, according to the needs of those listening.

STORIES FOR SPECIAL CHILDREN

Stories have been used in other ways too. Parents, grandparents and older children have invented characters and developed stories for their offspring and younger siblings. Many of these stories, despite success within the family, never reach print. However, some do, and these often become classics. Charles Dodgson (Lewis Carroll) wrote *Alice's Adventures in Wonderland* for Alice Liddell; Kenneth Grahame's son was the inspiration for *The Wind in the Willows; The Hobbit* was written to be read aloud; *Watership Down* was written by a father for his children, and A. A. Milne gave life to his son's toys in the prose and poetry of the books about Christopher Robin and Winnie-the-Pooh.

Many written stories began life as oral tales.

Well-known folk tales such as *Cinderella, Jack and the Beanstalk,* and *Little Red Riding Hood* have their counterparts in many European languages. Across the world the same oral stories appear and reappear. There are 37 known variations of *Cinderella*! The tales of Johnny Appleseed in America and Granny Smith in Australia have similarities, as do the lumberjack stories of Paul Bunyan in America and the tall tales or yarns of the Australian timber country.

Today's children, living as they do in a multi-cultural society, are growing up with the stories of ethnic groups other than their own, and no doubt future adaptations will be a set of stories which will come from this period.

Cinderella *has been "told" in countless versions throughout the European and English-speaking world. First published in a spicy adult version in Italy in 1634 by Gimbattista Basile, it was told by the Frenchman Charles Perrault during the reign of Louis XIV and illustrated by Gustave Doré in 1867* (**left**). *Jacob and Wilhelm, the brothers Grimm, told an early folk-tale version in their* Household Stories *of around 1812, illustrated here by George Cruikshank, in the first English edition* (**center**). **Far left** *This elegant but still moral version was published in 1919, and accompanied by some of Arthur Rackham's finest illustrations. By the mid-20th century, Cinderella had become just another skin-deep soap-opera character* (**above**).

THE BUSINESS OF STORYTELLING

Stories are a part of life. The anecdotes an adult brings home from work, the stories heard in the shopping center, the events which take place on a child's way to and from school, are all stories, told and retold, embellished, polished and held up for the listener to remark on. Anywhere and anytime is the right place for a story. Formal storytelling usually takes place in libraries, schools, care centers, parks and backyards. Informal storytelling can take place anywhere: at home, in the car, on a train, bus, or airplane.

Who should tell stories?

In some communities in certain countries there are people who are designated the official storytellers for the community. But in most societies anyone can tell stories; all that is needed is a willing teller, a good story and an audience. However, each teller should be aware that an individual style is needed. Good storytellers are those who do not imitate another's style, especially not someone else's telling of a particular tale. Tellers should develop a repertoire of stories for varied occasions and be able to select stories to suit the audience.

Watch for danger points:

Be aware of your own limitations, and don't attempt to tell stories well beyond your own experience.

Be wary of telling stories from another culture – especially if they require a special dialect, accent or a specific method. Unless you are *very* good at imitations, such tellings may result in a "dead" story and a disappointed audience.

Choosing a story to tell

Formal storytelling does need some degree of selection. The teller needs to know the intended audience, to be aware of the likely age and experience of the audience listening. A storyteller should use only stories she or he is comfortable with and knows she or he can tell with full understanding, feeling and belief. Most storytellers find that a particular form or genre of story suits their telling style best. This might be traditional folk tales, stories from a particular culture or country, modern stories, humorous stories, ghost stories, or adventure tales. Whatever the form of story chosen it must be right for the storyteller and the audience.

Right *J.R.R. Tolkien's own drawings for* The Hobbit, *give another glimpse into the author's imagined world for both reader and listener.* **Opposite page** *One of Eileen Colwell's wonderful reading-aloud collections,* More Stories To Tell, *has springy black and white drawings by Caroline Sharpe.*

.The ElvenKing's Gate.

Are there stories that always work?

Donald Bisset has written a number of collections of stories for children. All are worth telling or reading aloud. Over the years they have been told by the author to many audiences. However, one story called *Nothing* might be difficult to find as the author uses it to gain the attention of his audience before launching into a longer story.

Eileen Colwell's collections are of stories she has told over many years. They are mostly traditional stories which she has developed to suit her own style and which she knows work well every time she uses them. This storyteller is world famous and there is one particular story which few other storytellers would dare to attempt but which she has made her own. *Elsie Piddock Skips in Her Sleep* by Eleanor Farjeon takes 40 minutes to tell, and told by Eileen Colwell it is a magical listening experience.

Many inexperienced storytellers have turned to well-known stories as a source of inspiration, and found that some are failures when told aloud. *Tom Tit Tot* and *Three Little Pigs* can be told by anyone, but time and again experienced as well as inexperienced storytellers have tried to use A. A. Milne's stories and failed. These are stories for sharing with one, two or three children, but not with a group of more than four. The stories are far too intimate. Conversely, *The Hobbit* by J. R. R. Tolkien is meant to be read aloud, not told, and works wonderfully well in the hands of an experienced and talented reader. Selecting stories for telling is a personal matter. No person can judge for another which stories will work on a particular day.

PREPARING YOUR STORY

Once you have found your story, the next thing is to learn it. The story should be read and re-read until it becomes a part of the teller. Each episode within the story should be broken down so that it is fully understood and the sequencing complete. The story should be read aloud, many times, taped and listened to, then read aloud again. The teller should check **the nuances in speech, the inflections of voice and the pace of the story. Words which are not easily understood should be substituted.**

No story needs to be learned by heart unless it is a story poem. *All stories should be learned for their content.* If the story sounds flat, try to work out why that should be so. If in doubt listening, rereading and retaping you cannot figure out what is wrong with the story, then the story should be discarded.

Every story must be learned thoroughly, and even after it has been told numerous times, it should be reread at source. It is surprisingly easy gradually to miss out some important though minor details of a story, and only rereading at regular intervals will keep the story whole and save it from turning into a totally different story from the one you began with. Every story should be prepared with a particular audience in mind. Not necessarily specific people, but an age group, an interest group or a type of listener.

TELLING THE STORY

Most storytellers develop their own style of delivery as well as their own style of story. The best way to find out what sounds right – how to pace a story, how to develop the story line for the audience – is to listen. You can tell the story to yourself in front of a mirror while taping it. Or, if this is inhibiting, you may prefer to tell the story directly onto tape and gauge the action and delivery from the pace of the story. Every storyteller should listen objectively to him- or herself telling stories, or tape a session and then criticize the delivery. In this way it is possible to eliminate extraneous words and phrases, unnecessary mannerisms in speech and action, and the overuse of an exclamatory remark before they become a habit.

Every storyteller must remain aware of the audience while telling stories and be prepared to alter a story if it seems that the audience is losing interest, has missed an important point or is simply not involved in the story. Changing a story while telling it demands a far greater knowledge of the story than a mere recitation of the words.

The same audience hearing the same story for a second or third time should not be able to tell which words are coming next, although they may know the sequence of the story. A stale story is one that is told in exactly the same way time after time. All storytellers must learn to embroider a story, to lengthen or shorten it for maximum effect and involvement of the audience. Children do this constantly when relating events from school to home and vice versa. Stories may need to be interrupted by the teller in order to explain some item, event or action which does not seem to be clear to the audience. It might be necessary to change the sequence of events so that the audience can understand more easily.

CAN I TELL STORIES THAT HAVE BEEN PUBLISHED?

Traditional stories – whether published or not – are outside the normal period of copyright *as far as the story itself* is concerned, although particular retellings of folk and fairy tales are in copyright to the reteller. Stories that have been written by an individual and that the storyteller uses as a told story are under copyright. This also applies to chapters or incidents from books that might be used by the storyteller.

To check this, look on the back of the title page. This page lists all information relevant to the book including what is called the copyright statement. Usually this will be, for example, "© Ann Author 1988." To contact Ann Author for permission to use and perform her work, the storyteller should write to the rights manager of the publishing company that published the book. The publisher's address should also be on the back of the title page, but if it is not there, check *Books in Print* for American books or *British Books in Print* for British books. Both are available in public libraries. Then write to the publisher with details of what is to be used, the place, time and date of the session in question, and a request for permission to use the episode, chapter or story. Some will charge a fee. However, many publishers will give permission and not charge, and some will not even require a formal application.

Paid performers of stories must apply to the publisher, not only for permission to tell the story, but also to inquire if a performance fee is payable. Often no fee is asked, but a formal request must be made and an answer received *before* the performance. Most authors, publishers and holders of copyright regard it as a compliment if a storyteller wants to use some material for which a copyright is held.

FROM SPEAKING TO WRITING ...

Storytelling should, above all, be a pleasure for both the teller and the audience. The lack of a book lessens the distance between teller and audience and promotes the intimacy that must have been known by those early community storytellers. The retelling of a story to an audience and the listening to a well-loved tale recreate the atmosphere of an earlier time and place.

Storytelling is a living tradition, practiced, revered and valued in many communities around the world. Without this oral tradition many stories would be lost, and without storytelling today children would lose some of the tales of their own cultures. Stories should never be limited to the "once-upon-a-time" kind but should include those of a nearer time – 50, 40, 10, 5 years ago and now, in terms of tradition and culture. And a storyteller who likes to tell his or her own stories to a live audience may well be among the best of children's book writers – those who write for reading aloud and those who can also write for an intimate one-to-one relationship with one single reader at a time.

Some aspiring writers might find their creative talents best used in telling stories to children either their own stories or those from other writers. This is not to say that told stories are not good enough for print but rather that the told story might not transfer into print until it has been tried and tested many times with an audience. Perhaps it will always be an oral story. Or perhaps at a later stage, when the author is an experienced storyteller, the time may come to write down a story which has been told and retold with success. By that time the storyteller will know exactly how the story works and be able to reproduce its special "tone of voice."

A last word of warning: once embarked on the trail of storytelling and the search for stories, it isn't possible to turn back. Once a story has been told to an audience and the teller has felt the power, the stimulation and the fun of sharing words, and the joy of spoken narrative, the teller and the audience are hooked for life.

Storytime is a recognized moment of group involvement and togetherness in schools all over the world.

Chapter 1

The Basics of Writing
for Children

I'm often struck by the enormous variety of the ways in which – according to their own accounts – writers get to work. Some say that they never put pen to paper without having worked out the whole plot beforehand. Some will have a vaguer idea of the outlines of the story and will "discover" its complexities and its resolution as they write. Others start with a character and allow the narrative to expand around that character's development. Some begin with an incident or a situation and then find that other events follow naturally, so that the story becomes continuous; or they may have found a pattern that can be repeated, with variations, to make up a book of short stories.

STARTING WITH A CHARACTER

Sometimes, by looking at the end product, we can guess which of these different methods was used by a particular writer; sometimes we have to rely on direct information from the writer himself. It seems likely that Patricia L. Spears embarking on her first story about "Angelina," A. A. Milne with Christopher Robin and Pooh, and Peggy Parish with her "Amelia Bedelia" stories realized that they had hit on formulas which, with variations, could be used time and again with great success. The successful formula in each of these examples depends on a central character whose idiosyncrasies dominate any situation in which the author chooses to place him or her: Angelina is a "bratty" young mouse who must learn all life's lessons the hard way; Pooh is a bear of very little brain, with a large stomach and a large heart; and Amelia Bedelia does everything backwards. An additional bonus is that in Patricia L. Spears' and Peggy Parish's stories, the disruptive behavior with which a child can identify is shown as funny rather than unacceptable.

Sometimes the idea of a clearly defined character can result not in repetitive incidents but in a long story with a beginning, a middle and an end. Frances Hodgson Burnett wrote: " . . . *one day I had an idea, 'I will write a story about him,' I said, 'I will put him in a world quite new to him and see what he will do . . .'.*" It was a good idea and, because she was already an experienced storyteller, Cedric Errol, the character based on her small son, accumulates round him the other characters and events that make *Little Lord Fauntleroy* a good, if now unfashionable, read.

This passage from Frances Burnett's autobiography suggests that she was one of those writers who begin with an unstructured idea of the plot, but who have an idea of a situation which demands development. Without knowing exactly where the story would end, the author must have first thought of Sara Crewe, the warm-hearted little rich girl who is suddenly reduced to extreme poverty but who behaves throughout like *A Little Princess*; or, in her best book, *The Secret Garden,* of plain, spoiled brat Mary Lennox, transported from her luxurious life in India to solitude and a harsher reality in cold Yorkshire.

Ernest Shepard's illustrations of two very different modern classics: Kenneth Grahame's The Wind in the Willows, *1931, and A.A. Milne's* Winnie-the-Pooh, *1926.*

STARTING WITH AN INCIDENT

Most writers know how an incident, read or heard of, a chance phrase or a casual meeting can spark off a conviction that this is something that will one day be the nugget of a book. It may take years for the necessary accretion to develop around it, but the idea remains, sometimes irritating because it is still unused, sometimes comforting because of its potential.

I had this experience when I heard that the Mother Superior of a convent, which was also an orphanage, had said that every child in her care had an "absent mother"; some of these mothers actually existed, but most were invented by the children themselves – on the principle, no doubt, that if your mother does not exist, it is necessary to invent her. I knew at once that this was one of those ideas that only needed time to germinate. Years later, I suddenly found a connection between this remark and the behavior of orphaned baby rhesus monkeys who, in experimental work by two American psychologists, were found to develop into schizoid, sexually immature adults if their mother-substitute was made of cold wire, but who grew up normally if these substitutes were made of something cuddly like soft terry cloth. Somehow, the psychological experiment fueled the Mother Superior's comment, and I wrote a short book, *Rufus,* about a boy living in an orphanage, who discovers, after many mistakes, how to construct the sort of fantasy mother who will support rather than destroy him.

PROMPTING FROM OUTSIDE

So far we have dealt with ideas arising spontaneously in the writer's mind; but ideas can be encouraged to take shape or actually planted in that mind by outside agencies. There can hardly be a parent living who hasn't at some point or other found it necessary to concoct a sort of story in order to amuse, reassure or soothe a child. Most of these "occasional" stories do not reach the public; by their nature, they are meant for a special audience, often tailored exactly to suit a given situation. Ask any editor of children's books how many unsolicited manuscripts are sent in every week, with the hopeful note saying "*how much my own children have enjoyed this,*" and you will hear what a tiny proportion are considered suitable.

Knowing this, we might well be surprised that any stories told to, or written for, one particular child can be successful, but there are splendid instances to prove that we would be wrong. *Treasure Island*, for example, was written for Robert Louis Stevenson's stepson; and to carry the argument a step further, Rider Haggard wrote *King Solomon's Mines* in direct rivalry with Stevenson. It seems likely that in all cases where an outside stimulus has sparked off a masterpiece, this is because the idea was lying there, like a dried-up seed, waiting to sprout. Then the child demands a story or the publisher asks for a book, and the request is like water poured on parched land. The buried seed comes to life and grows into a flourishing plant.

Other people's ideas

Friends, and occasionally publishers, sometimes produce an idea which they think would be ideal for a writer to use as a starting point. I am not sure if this can ever result in a worthwhile story unless the writer recognizes the idea as one which fulfills his or her own need. This isn't always possible; there is, for instance, the formula often given to commissioned writers of romantic fiction – Boy meets Girl, Boy loses Girl, Boy finds Girl. It isn't exactly an inspiring brief! Or there are the editors who want a book for a specific purpose: "*Could you write something about a handicapped child in a deprived environment?*" "*We would like a story illustrating the problems of the single teenage parent, perhaps one in a racial minority group.*" It is very tempting and flattering to be commissioned, especially when you are young and struggling; but the process of fleshing out a ready-made skeleton is as different from the germination of the writer's own instinctively chosen starting point as is the work of a taxidermist from the development of the baby in the womb.

STRUCTURE

Having had the idea for a story, we then have to consider form.

Plotting in advance

Iris Murdoch is a writer who works out her plots in considerable detail before she begins to write so that she has a conscious pattern to follow as she adds the dialogue, the descriptions and the contemplative passages that make her work so remarkable. And just to confuse matters, Enid Blyton once described her way of writing as being like the transcribing of a series of moving pictures, which told her what was happening in her narrative. It sounds dangerously like inspiration; but as one musician wrote more than 50 years ago – apropos of the words of hymns – there are different levels of inspiration. Fluency and a sense of plot do not constitute genius, though they may add up to an agreeable amount in the bank.

Plotting from the inside

Not every successful book for children is a rounded story, with a beginning, a middle and an end. Many are more linear, a series of adventures, which don't really deserve the name of a plot. This works perfectly well as long as the events are sufficiently amusing or exciting or both. For example, in both of Carroll's *Alice* books the inconsistency of the chain of events is the negation of strict form but in keeping with the dream framework; and the strangeness and wit of each of Alice's adventures may compensate many young readers for the lack of a regular pattern. I myself did not feel this as a child. I resented the discovery at the end that the whole thing was a dream, and I missed the sense of development and resolution which more compactly shaped stories supplied.

Clearly, if you devise the whole of your plot before you begin to write, you will be able to ensure that your beginning leads on smoothly to the middle and that the end is an outcome, surprising or not, of what has gone before. If you start only with a situation, you are likely to have to do a fair amount of revision as you proceed. I have very seldom written a first chapter that did not have to be changed and often scrapped altogether. This is so usual that I've now come to consider the opening chapter merely as a way of getting started. Then, as the narrative opens itself out, I may find that one of the characters would act with more conviction if presented differently.

For instance, when I began to write *The Castle Boy* all I knew was that the boy imagined himself to be a hero living in medieval times. He was to find himself in a modern hotel, built on the site of an old castle and, at given moments, be transported back into the years of the Scottish Border wars and would discover that his heroism was more fantasy than real. But while I was writing, I realized that, if the boy were an epileptic, the "unreal" events could be synchronized with his seizures, so that the suggestion of magic – which was unsuitable for the age of the reader – could be eliminated. During their seizures, many epileptics are "out of time," which was just right for my story. This discovery entailed the necessary rewriting of most of the first half of the book.

Another common reason that may force the writer to revise what he or she has already written is the realization that an event which occurs in the middle or latter part of the story needs some sort of clue or suggestion leading toward it earlier on. For example, if, in Chapter 16, Dad and Mom decide to separate, there should have been some indication beforehand that all was not well with the marriage; it should be possible for this to have been conveyed to the reader, even if every character in the book is to be taken by surprise. But the breakup of the marriage may not have been in the forefront of the writer's mind when he began writing what he thought

(*Cont. page 22.*)

The story of Cinderella has been passed down through the generations. Each new telling reflects the culture and climate from which the retelling springs. However, the essence of the story — its content — remains the same — against her relatives' wishes, Cinderella goes to the ball where she meets the prince whom she subsequently marries. The four different tellings shown right represent a broad range of styles. Each version is very different, though the basic ingredients are the same. From top to bottom the tellings are Perrault's version (1692); the brothers Grimm (around 1812); C.S. Evans in a Heinemann version to accompany the illustrations of Arthur Rackham, published in 1919; and a modern telling published by Collins to accompany stills pictures from the Walt Disney cartoon of Cinderella. The telling by the Grimm brothers is bloodier than the others, ending on a note of vengeance; the Perrault original is a highly moral tale — with the moral printed at the end. Perrault saw it as a lesson presented in a particular short, dramatic way. To add to it — to change it — would overbalance the delicate structure.

BEGINNINGS

"Once upon a time there was a worthy man who married for his second wife the haughtiest, proudest woman that had ever been seen. She had two daughters, who possessed their mother's temper and resembled her in everything. Her husband, on the other hand, had a young daughter, who was of an exceptionally sweet and gentle nature. She got this from her mother, who had been the nicest person in the world."

"Once upon a time the wife of a certain rich man fell very ill, and as she felt her end drawing nigh she called her only daughter to her bedside, and said, 'My dear child, be pious and good, and then the good God will always protect you, and I will look down upon you from heaven and think of you.' Soon afterwards she closed her eyes and died. Every day the maiden went to her mother's grave and wept over it, and she continued to be good and pious; but when the winter came, the snow made a white covering over the grave, and in the spring-time, when the sun had withdrawn this covering, the father took to himself another wife."

"Once upon a time there was a nobleman who was married to a sweet and beautiful lady. They had one child, a little girl named Ella, and they lived in a big house..."

"Once upon a time there was a girl named Cinderella.
She lived with her stepmother.
The stepmother did not like Cinderella.
She made her work very hard every day."

MIDDLES	ENDINGS

"'Oh, yes, but am I to go like this in my ugly clothes?' Her godmother merely touched her with her wand, and on the instant her clothes were changed into garments of gold and silver cloth, bedecked with jewels. After that her godmother gave her a pair of glass slippers, the prettiest in the world. Thus altered, she entered the coach."

"Cinderella was as good as she was beautiful. She set aside apartments in the palace for her two sisters, and married them the very same day to two gentlemen of high rank about the Court.

MORAL: Beauty is a treasure rare.
Who complains of being fair?"

"As there was no one at home, Cinderella went to her mother's grave, under the hazel-tree, and said, –

'Rustle and shake yourself, dear tree,
And silver and gold throw down to me.'

Then the Bird threw down a dress of gold and silver, and silken slippers ornamented with silver. These Cinderella put on in great haste, and then she went to the ball."

"…but the Prince took Cinderella upon his horse, and rode away; and as they came up to the hazel-tree the two little white doves sang…
And as they finished they flew down and lighted upon Cinderella's shoulders, and there they remained; and the wedding was celebrated with great festivities, and the two sisters were smitten with blindness as a punishment for their wickedness."

"'Bless my soul, I forgot all about the dress!' cried the old woman; 'but that is easily attended to.' She touched Cinderella lightly on the shoulder with her stick, and immediately her dingy gown was changed into a magnificent dress of white silk, embroidered with butterflies and flowers of a delicate blue, and sewn with seed-pearls. Round her neck was a necklace of pearls and diamonds, and, greatest wonder of all, on her tiny feet was a pair of glass shoes, the prettiest that ever were seen."

"As soon as she was settled down, Cinderella sent for them [her stepsisters] and gave them each a suite of grand apartments at the palace. Not long afterwards they married two gentlemen of the Court, and Cinderella and the Prince lived very happily together for the rest of their lives."

"She waved her wand again.
Cinderella looked down.
Her dress turned into a white gown.
Her shoes turned into glass slippers.
'Oh, thank you,' said Cinderella."

"So Cinderella went to the palace
and married the Prince.
And they lived happily ever after."

was going to be a teenage love story; he will have to backtrack and insert his clues cleverly so that the information given does not seem out of place to the reader at the time.

Writers of detective stories must constantly have to do this sort of revision; the most ingenious of them can hardly foresee, as they write the early chapters, every clue that needs to be laid so that the reader will not feel cheated when he reaches the solution.

It may seem that writing that is started without detailed planning of the progress of the whole plot could not possibly result in a story with any recognizable form; but, surprisingly, it can and does. This structuring is, for many writers, largely unconscious; it's as if they have a not very exact blueprint just beyond the conscious working of the mind, and that what they introduce into the story tends toward the reproduction of that whole. I have sometimes found that an object or an incident which I thought I had "invented" to add some necessary realistic detail to a narrative has turned out to be an absolutely integral part of the plot. I also find that I know, all through my writing, that I can tell almost exactly where I am in the narrative, whether it is a quarter, half or seven-eighths of the way through. And if I depart too widely from those unconscious instructions, I become uneasy; I may persist, typing pages of incident or dialogue that seem perfectly relevant, but in the end I have to submit to that insistent voice which says, "*You are going in the wrong direction. Go back to page X, and start again.*"

It can be a maddening process.

Finding the right names

Another problem I have every time I begin a new story is what to call my characters. I can't feel comfortable until I've got their names right. Sometimes I know immediately that my hero couldn't be anything but Robert or that my heroine has to be Lucy, but there are times when I'm totally stuck. Then I read through the television listings for first names and the

DISCIPLINE

Perhaps this is a good point at which to emphasize that if you genuinely want to write a worthwhile book you have to be stern with yourself. It is fatally easy to pass something which isn't entirely right because you are tired of working, fed up with the whole project and because you feel you've put in so much time and energy that it ought to satisfy you – and your readers. But if you do this, you risk making your book very much less good than it ought to be. I don't want to imply that writing is always hard work, because sometimes it isn't; there can be hours when it flows and it feels and is right, but there are other hours when it's a slow, painful slog. One of the skills all writers have to learn – often through a good deal of "trial and error" – is how to piece together these differently achieved parts so that they make a coherent whole.

telephone directory for last names. This can be a snare, because sometimes I meet an inspiring name which doesn't fit this particular book, and instead of getting on with the work in hand my mind darts off into other pastures where this delicious new personality could wander. It is a good idea to name unpleasant fictional characters as anonymously as possible; it's best to call them Smith or Jones. You may think you've invented a name which no one could possibly have, but it's always possible that there really *is* someone called just that who will resent being portrayed as a "baddie" and may even think it worthwhile to sue you for libel.

SOME NOTES ON STRUCTURE

Plot

* Remember all books start with an idea: it might be simple or complicated.
* It doesn't matter what kind of story you are are proposing to write, plots fall into three categories: virtue triumphant the growth of the hero, when faced by situations that require moral choices the quest.
* Always keep in mind what kind of story yours is and make sure everything that happens in it is consistent with what you're aiming to do.

The beginning

Beginnings of books are particularly important when you are writing for children.

* Give the child reader enough information to know what line of story it is (family, animal, historical).
* Tell them something about the characters (a name, an age, a kind of animal).
* Hint at the setting (a house, a town, a mountain, an imaginary land).
* Aim to move into the action in an interesting way, providing information about the kind of book it is but at the same time making the reader ask questions that will entice him on to reading more.
* Resist the temptation to cram in too much information at the beginning. Ask yourself What does the reader need to know? Only include the essentials, the rest can wait.

The middle

Middles can cause lots of trouble. This is where the writer can lose impetus and the plot goes soggy.

Ask yourself:

* Is your story episodic? Is each chapter almost a short story in its own right, although each chapter is about the same characters who are moving toward a definite end?
* Is your story a split adventure? Do you propose to take some of your characters off on one series of adventures, and the rest on another, bringing them all together at a critical moment at the end? Are you going to switch from story to story at the end of each chapter? Or are you going to divide it up into larger sections?
* Is your story a single adventure? Is your hero faced with one problem or a series? If a series does the solution of one problem lead on to the next?

The end

Ask yourself:

* What is your end going to be? The finding of the treasure, the end of a life, the solution to a problem, peace after a storm?
* What kind of end do you want? Wholly or partially resolved? Is this appropriate?
* A happy ever after ending can be important if you are writing for younger readers and is expected if you write certain traditional forms of story, such as fables.
* For other types of books, endings do not have to be wholly resolved.

The author Troy Alexander wrote this checklist/memory-jogger of questions to ask yourself and points to remember when structuring a story. Experienced writers take on these points instinctively, for the writer starting out they are well worthwhile bearing in mind.

Change of direction

I'm always fascinated to find that – whether I know more or less what direction the story will take or whether I start with no more than a vague sense of its shape – there is a momentum that grows with the accretion of words on paper. It would be interesting to know – but difficult to discover – how many novels for children or adults have started out meaning to be one thing and have turned into something else. I have sometimes found that a story that I'd thought was going to have a leaning in one direction has turned out to be largely about something different. When I embarked on writing *The Chinese Egg*, I had seen it as a thriller concerning two teenagers who, for some inexplicable reason, find that they occasionally have glimpses of future events. What I had not foreseen was that the problems of teenagers with their parents and of the heroine's being an adopted child would play an important part in the story.

An illustration by Harry Furniss for Sylvie and Bruno, *Lewis Carroll's hilarious tale, published in 1889.*

MY CHARACTERS RUN AWAY WITH ME...

It may be the momentum of writing well during a good "session" – a wonderful feeling so long as it doesn't obliterate a sense of pace – which sometimes leads a writer to say: *"My characters run away with me, they seem to take over what happens in the story."* This won't do. The writer must be in control of the material; but, at the same time, he or she must not be deaf to the demands and to the voices of the characters who have been created. They must not act or speak in a way that will invalidate their identities or destroy credibility in the parts they have to play. The writer has, then, a double role.

1) The writer must constantly exercise a conscious critical faculty that tells him whether the story is going in the right direction and whether he is making his points clearly; this faculty will also monitor his style and his choice of words and phrases, analogies and metaphors.

2) At the same time, the writer is accommodating the flow of his or her narrative to fill out and to accord with the personalities of the actors chosen to play in it.

This holding of two functions – one active, at the front of the mind, the other passive, attempting to let what has already been created influence what is still to be written – is one of the most difficult of the writer's tasks. It is often tempting to impose a pattern that is passable, but not completely right, because it is easier and takes less time than to be still and to listen to the promptings of the spirit of the work in hand. This perhaps sounds pretentious when applied to writing for children, but there is no reason why young readers should be deprived of the best; that is, books that have the consistency inherent in the fusion of the author's intelligence and power of feeling.

DIALOGUE

Over the last 30 years the dialogue in books for children has become sparser, more economical, probably as a result of television. Television program-makers know that, if they are to hold their audience, an instant appeal for attention has to be made within seconds of the opening and that the action thereafter must be swift. While writers of the 20s, 30s and 40s could afford to start a book with a description of the family and the setting, present-day books for older children tend to start in the middle of the action, leaving the background of the narrative to be picked up from the ensuing conversation and events.

But these swift-action books are written for children to read to themselves; for younger children, who are more likely to be read aloud to, the slower start is not only acceptable but even better, since the listeners will want to have a clear idea of the setting of the story before the action starts and may also find it more difficult to pick up clues later.

Present-day dialogue is not only briefer, it is also more like that written for the stage or screen and much more realistic. It remains essential, however, to give each character his own recognizable voice, so that, even in a quick exchange of question and answer, the reader gets the feeling of the character speaking. But there's another trap here. If you listen to real-life dialogue, you quickly realize that to translate that exactly onto the written page is impossible. People hesitate, forget names, repeat themselves and, above all, introduce subordinate clauses that are perfectly understandable when said in a certain tone of voice, but are difficult to understand and too lengthy when read. You have to find a way of translating this so that it's acceptable. It's possible to have one character who speaks in sentences full of parentheses:

"Yes, I went grocery shopping on Wednesday (no, it must have been Thursday, because I wanted to buy fish for dinner on Friday) and I remember thinking I must take my umbrella because the morning forecast had said it was going to rain (in fact a storm, they said . . .)."

This, then, becomes a characteristic of that speaker but can't be used for others, even if this is how most of us talk. You must impose on most of your characters a manner of speaking that sounds realistic, although, in fact, you may have cut out half the words they would really use.

I once had an interesting example of the importance of fitting the dialogue to the speaker. I found it necessary to change the sex of a child in a story I had written: a girl had to become a boy. I discovered that this involved not just the substitution of a name and of the pronouns, but also of every sentence the child uttered. It wasn't that the language was so different; it was that a brother's attitude toward a younger sister is not at all the same as an older sister's to that same little girl; what he said had to be in keeping with his new personality.

DO'S AND DON'TS OF DIALOGUE

Do make sure the reader knows who is speaking.

Do give each character his or her own "voice."

Do give your characters realistic speech patterns.

Do edit "lifelike" speeches to work on the printed page.

Do ensure that dialogue is always appropriate to the speakers involved.

Do allow your characters to reply to *implied* as well as direct questions.

Don't let conversations go on and on . . .

Don't let your character's dialogue "run away" with the story or hold up the action.

THE CUCKOO TREE
by Joan Aiken

"'That he can,' Dido agreed. 'Ask me, he has his head in the clouds most o' the time, he's got some right cork-brained notions. And that old witch as sees arter him – Sannie or whatever she calls herself – it's a plaguy shame she couldn't be shipped back to Thingummy Island, her and her Joobie nuts.'

Gusset glanced round him warily. 'You're right there, missie,' he said, sinking his voice.

'What are those Joobie nuts, anyways?'

'Summat she brought with her from Tiburon, Missie Twido. She grows 'em from seed, up where the old asparagus bed used to be. She allus has a-plenty of 'em. Don't you go a-swallowing they hampery things, missie - they'll give you the hot-chills, don't they give you wuss.'

'What happens when Tobit comes of age next week?'

'Why, nothing much, missie. I reckon things'll goo on pretty much as usual.'

'He doesn't come into any cash, so's he could go off to school?'

'No, missie. Only the Heirloom.'

'What's the Heirloom?' Gusset had spoken as if everyone would know of it."

Note the clever planting of the exotic features that convey Sannie as a considerable force but of unknown strength.

Gusset has had some education, and a position to maintain, and only occasionally displays his country origins. This is most marked when he gets excited about Sannie.

We are given a subtle indication of Gusset's attitude towards Dido. He treats her with respect.

Dialect should be used with care. Too much on a page is off-putting to a young reader, who will be puzzled and confused by strangely spelled words. But used carefully it can add flavor and character.

It would be easy to embark on a discussion about the dreadful effects of the Joobie-nuts. Instead, we – and Dido – have absorbed some crucial information, and the dialogue moves us on smartly to the next critical piece of information.

By this stage in the book, the characters are well established with their own voices. They can talk to each other without Aiken having to indicate who is speaking each time.

The dialogue between Dido Twite and Mr Gusset the butler in Joan Aiken's *The Cuckoo Tree* is a good example of how the idiosyncrasies of character can be expressed through speech. It is a marvelous combination of the humorous and the sinister – reminiscent of Dickens.

FINN FAMILY MOOMINTROLL
by Tove Jansson

Do you expect a boat to be this color? It lends a note of the unusual to the unusual situation being discussed.

Dialogue does the work of describing the action. This is a useful method of moving the plot along.

" 'They've found a boat!' cried Snufkin. 'Come on! Let's run and see!'

It was true. A lovely big sailing-boat, complete with oars and fishing-tackle, and painted in white and mauve!

'Whose is it?' panted Moomintroll when he had reached them.

'Nobody's!' said Moominpappa, triumphantly. 'It has been washed up on our beach, so we have a right to keep it as wreckage!'

Note how excitement is conveyed by the use of short sentences and all the characters speaking almost simultaneously.

'It must have a name!' cried the Snork Maiden. 'Wouldn't *The Pee-wit* be rather sweet?'

'Pee-wit yourself,' said the Snork rudely. 'I prefer *The Sea Eagle.*'

'No, it must be Latin,' cried the Hemulen. *'Moominates Maritima.'*

Note the words and phrases which convey the sense of children jostling for position and being rude to each other in a friendly way to gain the best position – in this case the right to name the boat. Most of the real information, and the decisions, come from the grownups.

'I saw it first!' squeaked Sniff. *'I* must choose a name for it. Wouldn't it be fun to call it SNIFF? That's so short and sweet.'

'Just like you – I *don't* think!' said Moomintroll, jeeringly.

'Hush, children!' said Moominpappa. 'Quiet, quiet! Obviously Mamma will choose the name. It's her excursion.'

This extract is only a few lines long – yet how much character is conveyed in the simplest, most economic way. We start with an exciting statement – and are invited to join in. The exchange of information quickly gets bogged down. Moominpappa must act as *deus ex machina,* and move the story on.

Moominmamma blushed a little. 'If only I could!' she said, shyly. 'Snufkin has such an imagination. I'm sure he will choose much better.' "

In *Finn Family Moomintroll* the characters gather in excitement because a boat has been found on the beach. Tove Jansson develops a logical and wholly believable world in her *Moomin* books. As each new person speaks, we have a perfect description in miniature of their whole character and outlook – Moomintroll is the curious boyish hero, Moominpappa the practical man of the world, the Hemulen learned, a little pedantic and so on.

THE STRANGE AFFAIR OF ADELAIDE HARRIS
by Leon Garfield

Note the author's use of particular words and phrases to convey a period atmosphere – there's nothing that a modern child would find difficult to understand, but taken together they convey a strong sense of another age.

Bostock's questions convey his slowness and confusion – Harris is using his verbal ability to manipulate – and probably con – his friend.

Each time Bostock asks a question, a bit more of the "plot" is revealed. Questions can be used very effectively for this purpose.

The repetition of the phrase "human nature" – a weighty notion – gives the impression of philosophical depth. All con men like to use the chance to impress their victims, and Harris is no exception!

Consider the names – Bostock sounds solid, heavier and slower than Harris, which is light and quick off the tongue. Another clever indication of character.

A nice touch of irony delivered effortlessly.

Contrast verbose Harris with Bostock's few words.

"'But I've thought of something, old friend,' whispered Harris reassuringly; in a curious way, Bostock's simplicity seemed to reassure both of them. Bostock's great faith gave Harris confidence, and the more confidence Harris displayed, the greater grew Bostock's faith. There was really no limit to it all. 'I think I know where she is.'

'Who?'

'Adelaide. I've put two and two together, Bosty – and there's only one answer.'

'What's that, Harris?' breathed Bostock, who was not strong on arithmetic.

'She's back in the school.'

'How do you know?'

'Human nature, Bosty.'

Bostock frowned; he did not like to question Harris, particularly about human nature.

'Mark my words, Bosty, at this very minute my sister's asleep at the school, snug in Miss Alexander's bed.'

'Then – then Ralph took her all the way back again?'

Harris tapped the side of his nose. 'Human nature, old friend. He fancied Miss Alexander; Miss Alexander fancied Adelaide. Two and two, Bosty.'

'Human nature,' nodded Bostock, but with a note of uncertainty in his voice. Then Harris smiled and Bostock was reassured.

'Let's go, Bosty.'"

In Leon Garfield's *The Strange Affair of Adelaide Harris* there is this wonderful exchange between his two young heroes – the comedian playing off his stooge. The quick, short, sharp phrases carry the plot along at a crucial stage, while firmly underlining its period flavor . . . .

THE PRINCESS AND THE GOBLIN
by George Macdonald

" 'I want to talk to you,' said Irene to the little miner; 'but it's so awkward! I don't know your name.'

'My name's Curdie, little princess.'

'What a funny name! Curdie! What more?'

'Curdie Peterson. What's your name, please?'

'Irene.'

'What more?'

'I don't know what more. – What more is my name, Lootie?'

'Princesses haven't got more than one name. They don't want it.'

'Oh then, Curdie, you must call me just Irene and no more.'

'No indeed,' said the nurse indignantly. 'He shall do no such thing.'

'What shall he call me then, Lootie?'

'Your royal Highness.'

'My royal Highness! What's that? No, no, Lootie. I won't be called names. I don't like them. You told me once yourself it's only rude children that call names; and I'm sure Curdie wouldn't be rude. – Curdie, my name's Irene.'

'Well, Irene,' said Curdie, with a glance at the nurse which showed he enjoyed teasing her, 'It is very kind of you to let me call you anything. I like your name very much.' "

Curdie's question underlines that he has never been taught to talk to princesses! He's polite, in his turn – but one does not ask princesses their names!

Irene, the princess, takes the lead in the conversation, as she will have been trained to be polite in every situation, and to be in command of any situation even one as unlikely as talking to a boy miner.

Lootie represents convention – here, outraged convention. She strongly disapproves of Irene talking to Curdie: she can't stop her, but she can let her shock and affront be perfectly clear.

Irene gently puts Lootie in her place by turning her title into an insult! The tables are nicely turned against convention.

Curdie's dialect is subtly conveyed by the order of the words rather than by strange spelling.

Curdie's apparently innocuous remark to Irene is a piece of mild sarcasm directed against Lootie.

In George Macdonald's *The Princess and the Goblin* the eight-year old princess Irene and her nurse demonstrate their different attitudes toward Curdie, the miner's son in the above conversation.

ILLUSTRATION: WHAT TO EXPECT

When you have written your story and it has found a publisher you will have the problem of illustration. Here, there is a vast difference in what is required by the younger and the older readers. Any average reader under the age of, say, 10 will probably appreciate and even need illustrations. A picture can stimulate the interest and imagination of the child who is not yet a fluent reader; not only this, but where there are several whole- or half-page pictures to spin out the text, he can more easily achieve the triumph of having read a whole chapter for himself. A child with reading difficulties may also find that the illustration actually clarifies the text for him.

There is a school of thought that holds that it is better for children to form their own images of the written word than to have these presented with the text unless the illustrator is a master of the craft. However, many young children need the stimulus of some sort of pictorial representation of what they read, even if they have outgrown the picture book.

An illustration reinforces the sense, and, if the artist is lively, may introduce a new element into the text. As writers, this is what we should ask for in our illustrators. Speaking on radio about his immensely popular "Thomas the Tank Engine" books, the Rev. Awdry said he had stood over his illustrator and told him exactly how and what to depict. And the illustrations are, indeed, entirely at one with the text; they *add* nothing to it. However, the illustrator all writers long to meet is the one who can take the text and, without radically changing it, make of it something of his own and thereby enormously enrich it. I've had examples of this myself, and I know that, although sometimes the first reaction is *"But that isn't what I meant!"* I came to see that the artist had paid me the highest possible compliment: finding what I had written a starting point for his own visual inspiration.

I'm against illustration for older children. This is partly because illustrated books for young or grown adults are out of fashion today, and we tend to see illustrated books as being "picture books"; a young person of 11 and over is likely to regard a book with pictures as being meant for a much younger age. Also, I believe that by the age of 10, children are capable of forming their own images as they read and that these will be as valuable to them as those imposed by an illustrator. To give a personal example: my mother read the novels of Jane Austen aloud to me when I was 11 or 12; the illustrator of our edition was a particularly insipid artist. I don't remember ever taking any of his illustrations for my own, except, possibly, as far as the dress of the period was concerned. I felt that I knew exactly what Elizabeth Bennet and Emma Woodhouse looked like; so much so that I can't now watch a television version of any of the Austen novels. (See also *Picture Books*, page 54, *Illustration – Building a Career in Children's Books*, page 68, and *Making A Book*, page 80.)

THE BOOK AS A WHOLE – CONSISTENCY

Lastly you must consider the book you are writing as a whole rather than as a sum of its component parts. It must hang together. You must not cheat your readers by suggesting at the opening that this is one kind of story and then giving them another. This doesn't mean that you cannot experiment with strange forms, as Alan Garner does in *Red Shift*. In this book, Garner varies the time, place and characters without warning from page to page, yet the story remains the same man's desperate fight for life and love against hostile fate. What I mean could be compared with the key of a piece of music; a composer writing an

NAME: the Prince
AGE: early 20's
APPEARANCE: good looking in a conventional way. Dark hair, ? eyes, middle height and we?
CHARACTERISTICS: strong, assertiv?
ACTIVITIES: affairs of state
FAMILY: father (the king)

NAME: Cinderella (or Cinders)
AGE: 14-16
APPEARANCE: exceptionally pretty, golden hair, blue eyes, a natural blush, slight physique.
CHARACTERISTICS: a dreamer, kind, shy uncomplaining, demure, forgiving.
ACTIVITIES: Works very hard.
FAMILY: Father, fairy godmother, evil stepmother, stepsisters. NB. her mother died when she was a child

Use of an index card file of physical and temperamental characteristics may help an author to keep track of characters.

opera on a tragic theme will not introduce the work with a merry overture, rather he will tell us from the start that we should expect strife and unhappiness.

The writer of a humorous book will begin in a cheerful mood – it was a mistake for the first Babar book to open with the death of the little elephant's mother; a book dealing with serious problems must make it clear at the outset that this is a serious book. For example, Suzanne Newton's moving story of the adolescent problems of a small-town family, *I Will Call It Georgie's Blues,* begins with the narrator, Neal, telling us that both he and his sister Aileen have to conceal their real natures from their dictatorial father, the minister of the local church. On page three we hear that they are supposed, as "preacher's kids," to behave in public better than anybody else; on page five small Georgie is asking "Do you think Mom and Dad love me?" and it's clear that Neal can't answer this. We are at once aware that this book is going to deal with hypocrisy and a struggle that will demand great courage and that may – and very nearly does – end in tragedy. This doesn't mean that a serious book can't include comedy, nor

that a mainly funny book can't have serious scenes, so long as the overall tone of the writing is consistent with the main themes. It's a question of being able to sustain a mood, or of being able to recapture it when you sit down at your desk after a time gap.

Write as you please

I have tried to make it clear that there are as many ways of writing for children as there are writers. Perhaps I'm prejudiced in believing that the very best children's books are produced by those who discover, however they may have started, that they are writing largely for themselves. William Mayne was once asked for whom he wrote his children's books, and he replied, "*I write for the child I once was.*" I'm not saying that to write for any other reason is wrong or won't be successful; but I doubt if any of the acknowledged geniuses in this field wrote their masterpieces entirely to please the young without discovering a childlike enjoyment of the works in their own minds. Someone has said that writers produce the sort of books they themselves like to read. This is, I think, something that the would-be writer should never forget.

Chapter 2

Some Classic Children's Fiction

What is a children's book? What constitutes a "book for children" as opposed to one for adolescents or for the middle-aged, or the elderly? Uniquely in literature, children's books are written, illustrated, edited, published, analyzed, and frequently purchased, not by their intended audience but by adults. So then, who is the ideal reader of children's books? Who should the novice writer be addressing?

KNOW YOUR READERS

Some writers may take the easy view that, "A children's book is a book children read," or enjoy having read to them. While the problem may be sharpest for the writer who has in mind himself or herself as reader or the self he or she once was, it also has to do with the writer's and society's view of "childhood."

This chapter focuses on certain notable writers – as originals in their own right, but also as writers within the traditions of American and British literature for children.

"Children are people!" says librarian Janet Hill emphatically, and with such a sentiment most would readily agree. However, if a writer or illustrator attempts to realize such a statement in his work, then thunderclouds of disapproval may well gather around his head. There are more adults *in loco parentis* of a child's mind than you can shake a stick at, and many writers have found themselves defending their work from those who see it as their duty to find a "purpose" in the reading provided for children.

Nina Bawden perfectly expressed the author's plight when she declared plaintively: *"I sometimes think the child I write for is entirely absent [from educationists' discussions on books for children]. How can I explain that my reader is a person so incalculably complicated . . . that all I can do is try to write the book I have in me, and let the reader make of it what he will?"* One must be sympathetic to her point of view, particularly in the light of the quality of her own work.

While any notion of a book for children must acknowledge the "intended" reader as well as the actual reader, on matters of literary merit they need no patronage or special pleading. It is unarguable that the genuinely good writers and illustrators for children require of their audience both concentration and what D.H. Lawrence called "an effort of attention." They are amply rewarded, for, as many writers, critics and teachers point out, a child whose interest *is* captured will battle his way through the most improbable text, often in noisy and impoverished circumstances.

CHOOSING YOUR WORDS

Any discussion of children's books will produce statements concerning the limits beyond which a children's author cannot – perhaps even should not – go. These will range from inhibitions upon language itself – "Make sure they will understand it" – to matters of content and character – "No pessimism allowed," or, more likely nowadays, "Only pessimism allowed, otherwise it won't seem real."

Where the first is concerned, it is rare for any child gripped by the deep structure of the text to be inhibited by its surface structure. Fairy tales use heavily formalized and often archaic language patterns that are intrinsic to their fabric and meaning. The same "feeling" for the shape and flavor of language is characteristic in many contemporary writers. As top children's writer Alan Garner has said:

"What words can tell my story? The words are the language, and every language has to translate its quality as well as its meaning. The words are more than the packing of a dictionary . . . The more simply I write, the more I can say. The more open the prose as a result of clarity, the more room there is for you, the reader, to bring something of yourself to the act of translating the objective story from my subjectivity to your own."

But "simple" does not mean simplistic nor banal, and it is this "clarity" and "openness," rather than any apparent limitation of vocabulary, that mark out the genuine writer, for anyone, but especially for children. Note, also, in Garner's statement, the assumption of the collaborative enterprise which is the writing and reading of a book. In their book *Teaching Literature 9–14*, Michael Benton and Geoffrey Fox asserted, *"The reader is invited to play a game devised by the author."*

The writers under consideration here are connected by their expectations of their readers and their assumption that few, if any, textual problems are likely to be critical to the enjoyment of their books.

CLASSIC BEGINNINGS

There are as many ways to begin a children's book as there are children's books. However, there can be little doubt that opening lines are very important. If you fail to grab a child's attention from the very beginning, you may lose a reader forever. Below is a selection of what I consider to be the best opening passages in children's books. They all work either by launching the reader straight into the book or by building up the story in the reader's mind before the book begins.

"The Iron Man came to the top of the cliff. How far had he walked? Nobody knows. Where had he come from? Nobody knows. How was he made? Nobody knows." The Iron Man. Ted Hughes.

"Once upon a time there were four little rabbits and their names were Flopsy, Mopsy, Cottontail and Peter. They lived with their Mother in a sandbank underneath the root of a very big fir tree." The Tale of Peter Rabbit. Beatrix Potter.

"Old Granny Greengrass had her finger chopped off in the butcher's when she was buying half a leg of lamb." The Peppermint Pig. Nina Bawden.

"The Island of Gont, a single mountain that lifts its peak a mile above the storm-racked Northeast Sea, is a land famous for wizards." The Wizard of Earthsea. Ursula le Guin.

"Squire Trelawney, Dr Livesey and the rest of these gentlemen having asked me to write down the whole particulars about Treasure Island from the beginning to the end, keeping nothing back but the bearings of the island, and that only because there is treasure not lifted, I take up my pen in the year of grace 17, and go back to the time when my father kept the Admiral Benbow inn, and the brown old seaman, with the saber cut, first took up his lodging under our roof." Treasure Island. Robert Louis Stevenson.

THE IRON MAN

Ted Hughes

THE COMING OF THE IRON MAN

★

The reader is thrust straight into the story, curiosity aroused. Note the very short opening paragraph which in the space of ten words poses lots of questions. Without using a single adjective, Hughes manages to conjure an immediate picture.

Text anticipates child's questions, then answers them. In so doing the author creates a mystery.

The Iron Man came to the top of the cliff.

How far had he walked? Nobody knows.

Where had he come from? Nobody knows.

How was he made? Nobody knows.

Repetition of key words sets up a rhythm which makes the book a pleasure to read aloud.

The anticipation builds up. The Iron Man is described using comparisons with everyday familiar objects. This serves to make him a friendly, accessible monster.

Taller than a house, the Iron Man stood at the top of the cliff, on the very brink, in the darkness.

The wind sang through his iron fingers. His great iron head, shaped like a dustbin but as big as a bedroom, slowly turned to the right, slowly turned to the left. His iron ears turned, this way, that way. He was hearing the sea. His eyes, like headlamps, glowed white, then red, then infra-red, searching the sea. Never before had the Iron Man seen the sea.

A simile which is humorous, surprising and very good.

The language mimes the actions – slow and deliberate like the Iron Man's movements.

The last sentence shows the Iron Man's vulnerability.

Sustaining the suspense. The language is simple, well chosen and extremely precise.

Words which may not be familiar can be understood in their context.

He swayed in the strong wind that pressed against his back. He swayed forward, on the brink of the high cliff.

Long sentence, short words in short phrases. Sentence length is varied which increases cadence.

And his right foot, his enormous iron right foot, lifted – up, out, into space, and the Iron Man stepped forward, off the cliff, into nothingness.

Children respond immediately because the book starts with a climax – the apparent destruction of the aptly named Iron Man.

CRRRAAAASSSSSSH!

THE STORY

The Iron Man arrives out of the blue, and proceeds to eat all the machinery, cars, trucks, barbed wire . . . . He is befriended by a boy called Hogarth who finds him a delicious scrap metal heap on which to live (bliss!). Then a giant monster with "a stomach as big as Germany" threatens the planet. The Iron Man challenges the monster to a test of strength. The Iron Man wins.

THE PREDICAMENT OF CHILDHOOD...

Where moral problems are concerned, the writers are up against more formidable barriers, although even here authors like Robert Cormier and Paul Zindel succeed in writing with honesty and directness. The moral problem is not simply one of suitability, but comes from certain deeply felt, cultural assumptions about childhood. In our culture, childhood is heavily romanticized: the conventional view of it is as a time and place of idyllic irresponsibility and security. Certainly much writing for children perpetuates this view – happy vacations with excitement and adventures every day, and delicious suppers to end it all. As critic Humphrey Carpenter says: "*Growing up becomes synonymous with the loss of paradise*," and many writers encapsulate this view, their leading characters remaining firmly pre-adolescent.

However, some of the writers whose work is most distinctive view childhood differently. They see it as a time when, as a child, you are helpless, disregarded, on the periphery of events that shape your world.

Philippa Pearce is such a writer. Kate, the protagonist in her novel *The Way to Sattin Shore*, has always believed her father to be dead. Indeed, not only is he dead but his tombstone in the churchyard shows that he died the day she was born, so the event is doubly significant. Gradually, through happenstance, she pieces together the truth – he is not dead, but equally not there, and the discovery confuses her and destabilizes her world to an acute extent. No one will explain and she feels unable to demand an answer, because she is "only a child."

"Kate was beaten – she knew it. Whatever she did now – however she rushed and shouted her way into the kitchen – she was only a child. They would not listen to her, pay any attention to her."

Philippa Pearce's work is resonant with this theme. In her book *Tom's Midnight Garden*, Tom is put to bed so that he can get his "ten hours' sleep":

" '*A child of your age needs ten hours of sleep. You must realize that, Tom. For that reason, you must be in bed for ten hours, as I have said. I am making clear to you, Tom, that Gwen and I wish you, entirely for your own good, to be in bed and, if possible, asleep for ten hours, as near as maybe, from nine o'clock at night. You understand, Tom?*'"

Similarly in Alan Garner's *The Stone Book*,

THE WAY TO SATTIN SHORE
BY PHILIPPA PEARCE

Kate lives in a happy family, accepting that her father is dead and buried in a grave marked by a tombstone. When the tombstone disappears the facts of what Kate knows gradually disintegrate, as does the trust in her family who have hidden the truth from her "for her own good." Her father's reappearance starts a whole new chain of events for Kate.

TOM'S MIDNIGHT GARDEN
BY PHILIPPA PEARCE

When Tom hears old Mrs Bartholomew's grandfather clock in the hall striking thirteen, he goes to investigate. He discovers the poky concrete yard has been transformed into a wonderful garden. The enchanted place is inhabited by a Victorian girl called Hatty. Over a period of time Tom gets to know her. Who is she? We never really know . . . But she looks remarkably like old Mrs Bartholomew did when she was a girl.

---

his main character, Mary, is to some extent at her father's mercy. In order to get her stone book from her father, she has to follow him through a maze of terrifying underground passages, tethered to him only by a filament of "bad ends" of silk and absolute faith in his judgment.

> " 'Then this is what we're doing,' said Father. 'So you listen. You're to keep the lucifers dry, and use only one candle. It should be plenty, let the silk out, but don't pull it, else it'll snap. It's to fetch you back if you've no light, and that's all it's for. Now then, you'll find you go down a bit of steep and then the rock divides. Follow the malachite. Always follow the malachite. Do you understand me?'
> " 'Yes, Father.' "

Mary's "Yes, Father" shows her utter faith in him, but also her total dependence.

For these writers, childhood is the condition of always being in the dark, overhearing, joining together threads and glimpses to make the pattern, and always, always having to trust. "Just do what you're told and don't ask questions," has more to do with most childhoods than the "loss of paradise."

It's here that interesting cultural contrasts

THE STONE BOOK
BY ALAN GARNER

A book about people and their relationship to each other. Mary and her father, a stonemason, explore the landscape which gives him his living. What Mary discovers in a secret cave at the end of a tunnel is the answer to where she belongs and why her family is so special.

begin to emerge – in the British tradition of writing for children, the world is very much a physical object, a place where children become creatures of the *natural* world; in the American tradition, by contrast, it is the *social* milieu which is the context for the narratives. Again and again in British books, the geographical setting for the events is central to the text – it becomes a kind of collective cultural metaphor for childhood.

THE NATURAL WORLD OF CHILDREN

The natural world means the country – in English connotations that implies hills, farmlands, marshes – anything that is not town. This has less to do with fantasy as such – with writers like Pearce and Garner in particular, the observation is realistic and acute – than it has with the English romantic attachment to damp leaves and wet grass. The country in English terms is where an "ideal" existence is led, and in many juvenile books the land belongs to the children, the houses and town to the adults.

For example, look at Philippa Pearce's book, *Minnow on the Say*. The title is indicative of the whole balance of the story; the protagonists are not really the boys Adam and David, but the boat "Minnow" and the river Say. Such is the quality of the writing that in reading the book we enter a cool tunnel of overlaying willows and bordering reed beds through which the boat and the river travel. Even the man-made structures which the boys encounter have by virtue of antiquity acquired the patina of natural objects.

There is always the implication that man and nature perform in a cooperative enterprise, and that time gives the world eventually back to nature, to be discovered by subsequent generations.

Such a view of the world shows man and nature in a continuous relationship of modification and change, of use and decay, of man-

One of Edward Ardizzone's evocative drawings for Philippa Pearce's Minnow on the Say.

agement and reclamation in which children are accomplices. In *Minnow on the Say,* Alan Garner's *The Stone Book* and Lucy Boston's *Green Knowe* series, all the characters have in common the pursuit of exploration and discovery, in which they, as children, have special entry into a landscape forgotten by adults.

Ideas such as these are hardly simple or childlike, and yet the skill of these writers seems to provide few problems for their young readers. Understanding is helped by way of the central character, who becomes both writer and reader. In *The Stone Book* we see Mary's world, which is also Alan Garner's, through Mary's eyes – we move with her from her perception of the world made by primeval forces and shaped by her father.

"Yet Father had looked at the way the trees grew, and felt the earth and the leaf-mold between his fingers, and had said they must dig here. And there they had found the hard yellow-white dimension stone that was the best of all sands for building."

The device is highly useful because it allows both internal and external images to be centered around the stable structure of a character, and permits explanation and speculation which then becomes part of the thrust of the narrative. This unifying of writer and reader in the medium of the main character is often dominant in children's books.

POINTS TO REMEMBER

It's almost impossible to pin down what it is that makes a children's book a children's classic. However, by observing first-rate writers, the novice author can learn a great deal.

- Don't begin writing for children because you see it as somehow easier than writing for adults. It isn't! There may be fewer words in a children's novel but there should be the same amount of passion and commitment.

- Do try to recall the wonderment of a really excellent book; its "un-put-down-ability" even though you'd been told seven times to switch off the light and go to bed. Keep that feeling in mind as you begin to draft your book!

- Don't underestimate the intelligence of your readers.

- Don't limit your vocabulary or write down to children. If your storyline is gripping, your readers will be hooked, and they will make any necessary effort to understand the language you have chosen to use.

- Writer Joan Aiken has likened children's fiction to thriller writing. Certainly the skill of being able to keep the reader in delicious suspense and wanting to know what happens next is critical in children's books.

- Do be prepared to confront complex issues and create worlds that are not necessarily safe and cozy. Remember, some of the most brilliant children's fiction deals with children who are powerless, isolated and afraid.

- A common device used by many writers is to show the reader the world through the leading character's eyes. This can help to convey ideas which a child might otherwise have difficulty grasping. Try experimenting with this form. But don't stop there! Experiment with various forms until you find the one that is the most appropriate for your purpose.

THE SOCIAL WORLD ... OF ANIMALS

American writers are often preoccupied not with the natural and physical world, but with its social milieu. Narratives, these writers imply, are made by people in relation to each other, and as such they are commonly marked by a delightful and ironic wit. The work of William Steig is an excellent example.

People hardly exist in his books, yet his stories are all about the social world. Not merely about the world of people at large, but about sophisticated urban society. Take *Dominic*. Do not let the fact that Dominic is a dog fool you for an instant – he is the quintessential man-about-town, even to his obsession with dressing appropriately for every occasion.

> *"He owned an assortment of hats which he liked to wear, not for warmth and shade or to shield him from rain, but for the various effects – rakish, dashing . . . "*

Dominic sets out to see the world. His story is marked by the variety of characters whom he encounters, and not – as might be expected if this were a genuine animal story – by the landscapes through which he moves. He even comes upon that example of urban violence, a gang, whom he defeats by his wit

and *savoir-faire* – both examples of social manners. Each animal he meets is a social type, although there is no shade of anthropomorphism in Steig's delineation of their natures. They are animals, because this allows Steig the license to make a play upon the absurdity of human moral and social mores. (It also, incidentally, allows the human reader to adopt a lofty stance!)

Beatrix Potter's work is similarly unsentimental but, in contrast to Steig's, her characters are genuine animals, existing in the countryside as real animals do. Even in her most urban story, *The Tailor of Gloucester,* the mice who stitch the buttonholes of the mayor's vest make their escape through the holes in the wainscot when the cat scratches at the window. Even Simpkin the cat is entirely feline: *"And still Simpkin wanted his mice, and he mewed and he stood beside the fourposter bed."*

The jackets and coats Potter's animals wear are decorative devices, to do with illustration rather than the narrative, and frequently such garments are discarded early in

Below left *The witty and wonderful Brer Rabbit, from the Uncle Remus stories of Joel Chandler Harris, provides an identification point for the reader — the timid victim who constantly outwits his tormentors.* **Below** *Beatrix Potter's Peter Rabbit, however, can only be himself when he is freed from his "disguise."*

the stories. In *The Tale of Peter Rabbit*, she tells us that:

> *"Peter was most dreadfully frightened: he rushed all over the garden, for he had forgotten the way back to the gate. He lost his shoes among the potatoes. After losing them, he ran on four legs, and went faster, so that I think he might have got away altogether if he had not unfortunately run into a gooseberry net, and got caught by the large buttons on his jacket."*

It's evident from this that, once freed from the irrelevance of human clothing, Peter is more capable, and he becomes trapped once more only by his unnatural clothes.

Abel's Island

For Steig's animal characters, the clothes are as essential a part of their portrayal as they would be in the case of human characters. Abel, the mouse and hero of *Abel's Island*, attempts to survive on an island. (An island on which, we notice, birds, insects and plants all abound, and which we might think to be a happy hunting ground for mice – but is Abel a mouse or a person?)

> *"He was still wearing Amanda's scarf. It was the only thing he wore that was not in shreds. He had had to discard his shoes and socks some time ago. His necktie had been used to help hold up his hammock. He removed the scarf from his neck and let the birch feel its wispy softness."*

Note the contrasts here: "He had had to discard his shoes and socks"; Peter Rabbit sheds his with relief. Where Potter's creatures may wear, perhaps, a small sample of human clothing – a dress, or a bonnet, or a vest – Abel wears an elaborate outfit, complete in every detail. It is not merely the range of this clothing which distinguishes him from Benjamin Bunny or Peter Rabbit, but his concern with it as part of the way he perceives his public presence:

> *"The state of his clothes disturbed him. Damp and lumpy, they no longer had style. That would be corrected . . . "*

ABEL'S ISLAND BY WILLIAM STEIG

Abel the mouse and his young wife are picnicking one day when they are caught in a terrible storm. Abel is swept away. He ends up marooned on an island. Thereafter his time is spent attempting to get off it. He meets various characters a friendly frog, an unpleasant owl. After many months, Abel decides to swim for it. He eventually reaches home bedraggled, humbled and changed for the better.

It is clearly inconceivable that Abel – Abelard Hassam Di Chirico Flint of the Mossville Flints – Abel, for short, could be seen less than immaculately attired. "Manners (and fashion) maketh the man." Abel sleeps in a hammock; Potter's rabbits "live with their Mother in a sandbank underneath the roots of a very big fir tree."

The point these contrasts make is that even when the same device is employed by two writers, their employment of them is different. For Potter, the English writer, the animal is the true and natural character; for Steig, the American, the dog and the mouse exist within a set of human values and the reader is allowed to read their adventures as human adventures; their animalness is entirely artificial, which allows a deliciously ironic view of humans to be portrayed.

Ingenuity is the hallmark of Steig. His style is full of rich irony, suffused with a kind of weary tolerance of the absurdity of the world at large. Yet it is redeemed from cynicism by the pleasure to be obtained from observing it. Steig's central characters move through a series of social encounters with a wide-eyed innocence at variance with the style and language in which they are described.

THE CHILD AS ANTI-HERO

The "Treehorn" books by Florence Parry Heide present us with Treehorn, the ultimate anti-hero of children's literature. While the children in British stories are often seen as vulnerable, they are nevertheless evidently valued and protected by the adults around them. To some degree, the adults' lives circle around the children's adventures. Treehorn, by contrast, suffers all the knocks that flesh is heir to, bemused by adult behavior which requires his participation while disregarding him. The "Treehorn" stories are examples of the child trapped in an adult world: his teacher tells the shrinking Treehorn, *"Well, I'll let it go for today . . . but see it's taken care of before tomorrow. We do not shrink in this class";* in another book, Treehorn's birthday is ignored because his father is so busy developing a theory of economy.

In the "Treehorn" books, we catch the memory of what it is to be Treehorn, while remaining safely ourselves. In Parry Heide's books (and in Steig's) the real world and the world of the story are dependent. The second is a precise microcosm of the first, perceived through a witty sensibility. On the other hand, the worlds created by the British writers Pearce and Garner exist outside our reality – the reader moves into the creation and sets it apart from his present existence.

Evident in Florence Parry Heide's books is the degree to which they depend upon social attitudes and behavior. The "Treehorn" stories have more to say at a social level about 20th-century Western society than most theses of anthropological observation, and the message is all the sharper for its understatement and subversiveness.

As an example, take Treehorn's interview with the school's principal, to whom he has been sent for jumping in the hall. (The explanation, had anyone bothered to inquire, is simply that the shrinking Treehorn can no longer reach the water fountain.) The principal immediately moves into "Teacherspeak":

THE SHRINKING OF TREEHORN BY FLORENCE PARRY HEIDE

A boy called Treehorn discovers that he is shrinking. No grownup not his mother, nor his father, nor even the school principal comment on this fact, other than to tell him to sit up. At the end of the day, Treehorn starts to turn green . . .

" *'I can't read this,' said the Principal, 'it looks like shirking. You're not shirking, are you, Treehorn?' "* Treehorn then gets a lecture for a sin he has *not* been guilty of until he says:

" *'It says SHRINKING,' said Treehorn, 'I'm shrinking.'*

" *'Shrinking, eh?' said the Principal. 'Well, now I'm very sorry to hear that, Treehorn. You were right to come to me. That's what I'm here for. To guide. Not to punish, but to guide. To guide all the members of my team. To solve all their problems.'*

" *'But I don't have any problems,' said Treehorn, 'I'm just shrinking.'*

" *'Well, I want you to know I'm right here when you need me, Treehorn,' said the Principal, 'and I'm glad I was here to help you. A team is only as good as its coach, eh?'*

The Principal stood up. 'Good-bye, Treehorn. If you have any more problems, come straight to me, and I'll help you again. A problem isn't a problem once it's shared, right?' "

Every child knows that feeling of an inexorable process moving into action, regardless of its appropriateness. Every adult similarly knows the panic of having to sort out an impenetrable mess, and the need to have strategies that will remove any problem as rapidly as possible, while maintaining a veneer of control and cool-headed management.

Treehorn is not the character with whom we live in the text, but the cipher to a brilliant commentary about the condition of being "grown-up." We observe Treehorn's resigned acceptance of the ignoring of his birthday, the lack of presents despite the evidence of his closet tidied to receive them, his mother's obsession with appearances and his father's with financial management.

In Parry Heide's later book *Tales for a Perfect Child,* the children have learned to bite back! Woe betide any adults who encounter Harriet the whiner, or Emily, subversive chewer of bubblegum! In life, these books seem to say, you survive by being a smooth operator, and you'd better learn fast! Our sympathy for Treehorn depends upon his *slowness;* he can only cope with situations in retrospect – like any of us who thinks up the *bon mot* just too late! Treehorn is everyman, which is why he appeals so universally.

THE MODEL OF CHILDHOOD IN BOOKS

There appear to be certain clear conditions which attach to the state of childhood in books. The first of these is sociability. Isolation is regarded as being an unnatural state for children, a feature apparent in the real world as well; parents worried about "only" children; teachers organizing "group" work. The word "loner" is pejorative and the ideal family in children's books is described as a circle of mutually supportive people.

Family stories

The quintessential family book is Louisa May Alcott's *Little Women.* Its opening section sets both social context and character firmly within the framework of the ideal childhood.

"'Christmas won't be Christmas without presents,' grumbled Jo, lying on the rug.
'It's so dreadful to be poor,' sighed Meg, looking down at her old dress.
'I don't think it's fair for some girls to have lots of pretty things, and other girls nothing at all,' added little Amy, with an injured sniff.
'We've got Father and Mother and each other, anyway,' said Beth contentedly from her corner. The four young faces on which the firelight shone brightened at the cheerful words…"

This opening section establishes not only the interlocking personalities of the leading characters, but also the whole milieu of ideal family life – a fireside around which this group customarily gathers, interdependence, exclusiveness and mutuality of experience and values. It is a world of security and intimacy, universal in its appeal. This book is also characteristic of the story for children in that the adult members of the group are on the

The close-knit family group typifies the novels of Louisa May Alcott: the four "Little Women" cluster around their mother as the book opens.

periphery of the events, signifiers of protection and love. It is generally true that where such stories are concerned, adults are used to mark out the boundaries of childhood – they reinforce the condition of being "a child" so that, whatever dangers appear in the narrative their limits are made apparent.

This is clearly demonstrated in the "Swallows and Amazons" novels by Arthur Ransome. Despite the fact that children camp out on islands overnight and sail alone by day, the setting is a lake surrounded by adult habitations, conveniently within hailing distance of dry socks and hot food. Meanwhile, the adults themselves remain tactfully unobtrusive. *We Didn't Mean to Go to Sea* is the darkest of all the novels, one of the least characteristic, though most interesting, for in the book the author allows the adventure to become realistic in its recognition of the risk which attaches to adventure.

Adults portrayed in "Swallows and Amazons" and similar family stories mark out clearly the state of childhood; it is, in L.P. Hartley's words, "a different country: they do things differently there." Adult conventions frame the freedom which is seen to be part of the ideal state of childhood – only children can climb trees, play in the countryside all day, be close to the world of "Lets pretend." Adults cannot (say these books) imagine and invent with the completeness and verve of the child, nor can they abandon such imaginings so freely; adults are busy – preoccupied by the world and its routines – whereas childhood invents its preoccupations at will. Adults are an essential authorial device which illuminates the idyllic state of the child and his companions, secure and free at one and the same time.

The child in isolation

In structure though not in ideology, the story of the lonely child is quite different from "family stories."

In *The Secret Garden* by Frances Hodgson Burnett, Mary Lennox is seen initially as an unpleasant, arrogant and resentful child,

The lonely Mary Lennox wanders through the empty manor house in Frances Hodgson Burnett's The Secret Garden.

physically as well as emotionally unappealing. Everything in the opening section of the book contrasts with the opening to *Little Women*.

"When Mary Lennox was sent to Misselthwaite Manor to live with her uncle everybody said she was the most disagreeable child ever seen. It was true, too. She had a little thin face and a little thin body, thin light hair and a sour expression. Her hair was yellow and her face was yellow because she had been born in India and had always been ill in one way or another. Her father had held a position under the English Government and had always been busy and ill himself, and her mother had been a great beauty and cared only to go to parties and amuse herself with gay people. She had not wanted a little girl at all, and when Mary was born she handed her over to the care of an Ayah…"

Mary is alone, accompanied by adults related to her only professionally for they are employed to care for her and are, therefore, beneath her in station; her welfare is their duty. Before they died her parents were remote figures, and she had no companions of her own age and culture. She is removed to a landscape – Yorkshire – which is cold, dark, forbidding and in total contrast to all she has known. There are few people to be seen and no beauty she is willing to acknowledge. She finds herself incarcerated in an enormous dark Victorian mansion, complete with staircase, silent carpeted corridors and heavy mahogany doors, all of them shut. She is denied the normal activity of children in such contexts (in books anyway), that of exploration, since she is forbidden to go anywhere except those few rooms which are hers, and even the formal gardens restrict her to the graveled paths. Above all, she is alone.

It is a picture carefully built up to portray the total isolation of a child. Mary Lennox is excluded, and it is only her total disregard for her own unhappiness which allows her to find the "secret garden" and with it, Dickon. From this point on the book becomes the conventional family story, and when Colin comes on the scene the group is complete.

At the extreme end of the isolated child tale lies *Marianne and Mark* by Catherine Storr. In it Marianne's dream world breaks the barriers of what is traditional in children's books. Here there are no intervening adults to say, "Tell me all about it," and show the nightmare up for the unreality it is. Marianne is trapped in a fantasy no one can break into.

We watch Marianne create her imaginary world until eventually the means of creation, The Pencil, becomes her controller.

" *'I can make things happen there,' she said to herself. 'I did it before. The lines I drew across the windows are exactly like the bars there. I'll get rid of Mark. I won't ever see him again.*

She had picked up the india-rubber eraser and had started trying to rub out the face at the window before she remembered that the pencil was apparently an indelible one, and couldn't be rubbed out."

So far it's still rational but there is a gradual blurring of the lines between the logical explanation – indelible pencils cannot be erased – and the inexplicable . . . .

. . . " *'So it's the pencil!' Marianne thought in surprise. 'It's the pencil that started it all!' "*

Marianne and Mark is a compelling and challenging novel, but is it for children? And so we come full circle to our opening questions, by way of no answers at all, but with some characteristics possibly agreed upon:

- Writers reflect the cultural values of their own particular literary traditions.

- Where writers for children are concerned, those cultural values are both social and literary, and the actual reader – who is also the ideal reader – has to be found over the heads of intervening adults with their implicit, yet powerfully felt models of childhood.

- Writers as good as those mentioned here share a view of their audience as intelligent, sensitive and demanding. They are truly, "Good writers for good readers."

MARIANNE AND MARK
BY CATHERINE STORR

Marianne's strange dreams coincide with her discovery of an old pencil. Everything she draws during the day comes real in her dreams at night. She creates Mark and the house where he lives. She also creates THEM – sinister standing stones which can see and hear. Mark is trapped in the house until Marianne with the help of the pencil engineers his escape.

Chapter 3

New Writing on Contemporary Themes

When you start thinking about writing for children today you may become aware that it is not an uncontroversial field: you may have read in the popular press that some education department or library has "banned" a certain book, or that a parents' group has protested about one; you may have heard terms such as "new censorship," "new criticism," or "bibliotherapy." Literature is no longer viewed as just literature – it also poses social questions. It is not enough for a book to be well written or to be beautifully illustrated. Social critics of children's literature are asking writers and artists to adopt another set of criteria as well, and that is what this chapter is all about.

SOCIAL VALUES

The first thing to be said is that the addition of social criteria to children's books does not mean the abandonment of literary and aesthetic ones. This is a common misunderstanding of what "social criticism" is all about. You may well come across sneering

The traditional images of grandparents, parents and children — sometimes stereotyped in a rigid and unrealistic way — have given way in recent years to a more open and personal view: grandparents are often young and active; fathers care for children and mothers work; and little girls can enjoy an exciting ride on their bicycles as well as a quiet afternoon with their dolls. People are far more complex than clichéd portrayals suggest.

comments from establishment critics of children's books to the effect that all we want are stories about black handicapped children whose mothers can fix car engines. If such a book came my way, I would use the same criteria to evaluate it as I would for any other book.

Unfortunately, a lot of aspiring writers think that if they home in on a contemporary social problem, they will automatically produce a book that is worth reading. A lot of books have been written with worthy motives, striving to be relevant to children in the 1980s, which have been poorly plotted, skimpily characterized or written by someone with no ear for language – social relevance guarantees nothing!

PROPAGANDA

People who are afraid of the new criticism, who see it as a threat to the freedom of the creative individual or as a new form of censorship, believe that it is in favor of propaganda writing for children. Their position is that children's books used to be safe and neutral and that now a lot of radical pressure groups are trying to politicize them. One literary agent called them " . . . *a task force from the alternative society . . .bully-persons with an ulterior motive.*" Often such critics cannot easily identify these pressure groups; they are a bugaboo, a product of the paranoia of those who think that books don't need to move on from what they were like in the golden age of children's literature earlier this century.

Most of the new critics are as opposed to propaganda writing as any traditionalist. They know that formula writing of any kind shackles excellence. But where they differ from the traditionalists is that they believe that children's literature *never has been neutral.* Literature was firmly centered in the middle class – in Britain at least – when the great classics were being written, which led to the acceptance of certain values as the norm. The solid middle-class virtues of Mole, Ratty and Badger in *The Wind in the Willows* were highlighted by the fecklessness of the undeserving stoats and weasels who spoke in the cockney accents characteristic of the London working class. This was recognized by Jan Needle in his sequel to the book. Jan Needle's *The Wild Wood* tells the story from the point of view of the underlings. E. Nesbit, who wrote wonderful stories with careless fluency, is almost

impossible to read aloud without modification to children today because of the way she talks about the dishonesty of the "servant-classes."

Alice, The Wind in the Willows, The Phoenix and the Carpet, and *The Hobbit* all deserve their status as classics but they are *not* value-free nor do they set an unquestionable norm of storytelling; they are the work of intelligent men and women of Britain's Victorian and Edwardian middle class.

CENSORSHIP

Hand in hand with the scare stories about how left-wingers are writing propaganda in the disguise of children's books comes the other calumny that they are censoring or banning the classic stories that make up our children's literary heritage. This has achieved the same status of popular myth as the one about bra-burning among liberated women. I have worked since the early 1970s with groups of people who were concerned about racism in children's books and about how sex-roles, family structures and social class were handled. All of these groups have been concerned with the promotion of *more* books – not fewer – so that genuine choice can be increased. Many of them have published lists of recommended books which are non-sexist or non-racist. Not one has ever published an index of books it did not favor.

Every librarian, teacher, editor or parent exercises some kind of selection about the books that they offer to children. Some adults select on the basis of strong moral opinions. But we also select books for children for all sorts of other reasons, some of which are personal prejudices. Some adults can't abide snakes or frogs or spiders, and wouldn't choose to give children any book containing those creatures. Others dislike anthropomorphism and reject books that feature animals in clothes. So it is perfectly reasonable for a teacher to decide that he or she does not want to use a certain book for a class because it contains some kind of racial slur or an implication about the inferiority of women. This is not censorship but a legitimate exercise of personal choice in an area where *some* choices have to be made. The same applies to what a librarian chooses to keep as current shelf stock (as opposed to what can be obtained on request) or an editor chooses to publish on a list of books for children.

"AWARE" WRITING

So, does this give you a lot more problems if you are thinking of writing a children's book for the first time? It shouldn't. Your writing comes from the same part of you as your conscious and unconscious attitudes of thought and speech, what Tolkien called "*the leaf-mold of the mind.*" Whatever has gone into forming your adult opinions will feed into what you write. If you believe that black people are inferior to white ones, or women inferior to men, or people with little money inferior to those who have a lot, or if you don't like Jewish people, this can show up in your writing for children, and so it should. The most an editor can or should do is to point out to you the implications of what you have written and ask if this is what you consciously want to say. If it is, you should both go ahead. The reading public is entitled to your *real* views, not a liberal sanitization of them. And, if you hold strong views, you should be prepared to defend them.

But most of us fall into the trap of the cliché (such as "fall into the trap"!). These language-fossils are accepted as phrases shorn of their original meaning and used as building-blocks without much scrutiny. Aware writers will want to analyze the composition of clichés, whether of thought or its expression, and not use them unthinkingly.

Stereotypes

Stereotypes are cultural clichés and children's literature is full of them. Some are in the writing, others in the illustrations. They represent short-cuts in characterization, so that an illustrator may choose to identify the mother in a story – even if she is a furry mammal – by giving her an apron and the father by giving him a newspaper and a pipe. This is an unthinking use of symbols, which the artist assumes will be unambiguous – a sort of minimal set of signals indicating male or female parental roles. Working-class women wear curlers all day, blacks have rolling eyes and big white teeth, and so on.

Cultural assumptions are always at their clearest in illustration, but writing carries its share, even if they are sometimes more subtly expressed. Women's intuition, black people's "natural rhythm" or sporting prowess, Asian people's grace, the solidarity of the working class – you see, not all stereotyping is negative, but it is never convincing. You always know you are in the presence of a scantily-realized character.

In the matter of race, illustration has been a problem, with few artists good at depicting ethnic minorities. America is way ahead of the UK here, with excellent illustrators of black people such as Ezra Jack Keats, Leo and Diane Dillon, Rachel Isadora, Vera Williams and Jerry Pinkney. But there are still too few on both sides of the Atlantic. You don't have to be a black artist to draw black people convincingly, but it can help. Among the leading children's book artists in this field in the UK are Errol Lloyd, Ann Strugnell, Lisa Kopper, Caroline Binch and Susanna Gretz, only the first of whom is black.

The "selection" process of what is appropriate can be absurd: (**left**) The Rabbit's Wedding *by Garth Williams was banned in America because it featured the marriage of a white rabbit to a black rabbit.* **Below** *Ezra Jack Keats' sensitive portrayal of black children in* A Snowy Day.

More than one lifestyle

In the last decade or so the campaign against social stereotyping in books has led to a greater range of lifestyles being shown in children's literature. Once racial, sexual and class stereotypes were challenged, other social issues naturally followed. Why were family structures so limited in children's picture books? Nowadays fewer and fewer families are of the two parents plus two children nuclear variety, and children's books in the 80s are beginning to reflect this. *Gorilla* by Antony Browne is one of many picture books showing a single father with his daughter. Louis Baum, in his *I Want to see the Moon, After Dark* and *One More Time*, never portrays a two-parent family. Author/artist Vera Williams shows mother, grandmother and daughter living together in *A Chair For My Mother, Something Special For Me* and *Music, Music for Everyone,* and they are a working-class, non-white family at that! But these are books written and illustrated from the heart and gut, not stale social propaganda.

More handicapped children are now appearing in children's books, sometimes as the central character, but this *can* sometimes cast them too much in the role of a problem to be dealt with. It is better when they are present in books, as in the community, merely as individuals in their own right.

Age is one of the most stereotyped areas remaining in children's literature. Grandparents can actually be pretty young, but they continue to be shown as white-haired figures in their 70s or 80s. John Burningham's *Granpa,* which was a prize-winning book, shows the typical suspenders and collarless shirt of a man born early this century. Grandmothers are usually dumpy and aproned. When I reached my 40s and realized that, if I had not been such a typically middle-class late starter about having children, I could have been a grandmother myself, I began to ques-

Left *Anthony Browne's one-parent gorilla family in* Gorilla. **Below** *Joanna Burrough's illustration of Mary Hoffman's black-haired track-suited Grandma.*

tion this image. I wrote *My Grandma Has Black Hair* deliberately to show how a typical grandparent of the 1980s, in her late 40s, differs from the storybook stereotype. Age is another way in which children's literature reveals middle-class attitudes.

My children's living grandparents *are* in their 70s (although neither of them looks in the least like the children's picture-book image of 70-year-old people). It is as if some middle-class writers and illustrators first assume that grandparents are all the same age as their own parents and then try to broaden the class image by adorning these elderly people with the baggy pants and roly-poly figures that belong to a certain set of stereotypes about the working-class.

WRITER AS MIRROR OR CATALYST?

When I first became concerned about the image of adult women in children's picture books and started talking to parents' groups, I often met the objection that books could mirror society only as it is. It wouldn't be fair to show women as airline pilots if there weren't any in real life. Beware of this argument! At the time I was merely arguing for images of women as check-out girls, waitresses, secretaries – *any* work role, however stereotyped or mundane, that took them out of the home and into the marketplace – or images of women as car-drivers, book readers, dreamers, real people in fact, rather than the 24-hour service station for husbands and children (complete with apron) that children's books assumed them to be. A middle-aged man at such a talk one evening in the mid-1970s, got up and said, *"But aren't all mothers of children under five at home all day anyway?"* He had no knowledge of the real statistics – his mental image, like many picture books of that era, was a reflection of social conditions that were well out-of-date.

If a writer or illustrator is just a mirror, then let what they reflect be the here-and-now, if the book purports to be domestic realism. But it was Shelley who first made clear an alternative role for the creative individual. It is not only poets who are *"the unacknowledged legislators of society"* – any writer or artist can move things on a bit by creating new images and stimulating new ideas. It is not their job to endorse the *status quo*.

BOOKS AS PROBLEM-SOLVERS

One of the tasks that a writer mirroring society can take on is dealing with various kinds of problem issues. Here the line between fiction and non-fiction is very fine indeed. Even very young children are offered what are called "situation books," about starting school, moving house, adapting to a new baby and so on. As children get older, more problems are pushed their way. Reflecting a variety of family structures *may* entail dealing with a variety of family problems – divorce, death, even violence. By the time you reach the teenage novel, you begin to understand the old joke about the grownup asking at the bookstore for a good book for a child and the salesperson replying, "What's his problem?"

If you are thinking of writing about social problems in a book for children, you probably want to consider at what age children are ready to face up to particular traumas. Death is something that children become aware of between the ages of three and four. They may meet it first through the death of a loved pet or perhaps an older family member. Most traumatically, they may experience it through the death of a sibling or contemporary. Very young children will talk cheerfully about the details of disposing of bodies and so forth in a way that makes their more sophisticated but more fearful parents cringe. There are various

Susan Varley's prize-winning Badger's Parting Gifts, (**above**) *while* (**right**) *Louis Baum draws from everyday life in* Are We Nearly There?.

books about the death of pets such as *I'll Always Love You*, which they can read without distress. A particularly good one on the theme of death is the prize-winning *Badger's Parting Gifts* by Susan Varley, which stresses how the dead live on in memory. But rather older children, for whom death is becoming more frightening, might find even that book too painful.

There are other forms of bereavement, of which divorce is the most common. Many of the books which reflect this aspect of society do it very heavy-handedly and you should aim to tread lightly if you enter this delicate area. Some are deliberately written as problem handbooks, and have down-to-earth sound-

ing titles, such as *Mike's Lonely Summer* or *How It Feels When Parents Divorce* by Jill Krementz. There is a need for such books to ease the isolation of the child in the middle of a family breakup, but they will not often be read by anyone *not* in that situation and will remain bibliotherapy rather than literature. More graceful is Louis Baum's already mentioned *One More Time*, in which a boy and his father return from an outing by train and we discover only at the end that Dad doesn't live with the boy and his mother anymore. Words such as "visiting rights," "separation" and "divorce" are conspicuously absent, but this poignant story – which tends to move adults to tears – is bound to make children who live with both parents ask questions about children who don't. That is literature performing one of its most respectable subfunctions – increasing awareness of the way in which the

Raymond Briggs' When the Wind Blows *found an instant audience among adults and children.*

Dr Seuss used his great talents for gentle ridicule and strong insight to capture the essence of the arms race in The Butter Battle Book *in 1984.*

world is full of plots and characters.

We already have books about nuclear war, of which the first, and still one of the best, was Robert O'Brien's *Z for Zachariah*. Robert Swindell's *Brother in the Land* has been a timely warning, and the internationally successful *When the Wind Blows* by Raymond Briggs has brought the issue to a wide age range of children even though it was not originally published as a children's book. "Dr Seuss" brought the arms race issue to the very youngest children in 1984 with *The Butter Battle Book* in which rival nations who butter their bread in different ways are brought to the brink of mutual annihilation by their chauvinistic determination to prove themselves in the right.

REALISM VS FANTASY

So far I've written as if realism is the only mode in which to write for children. Fantasy in all its forms – whether animal fable, science fiction or the creation of other secondary worlds *à la* Tolkien – is another possible option. Of course, you don't avoid social issues by writing fantasy – they just appear in different forms. The great writers of fantasy for children this century – among them C. S. Lewis, J. R. R. Tolkien, Ursula Le Guin, Norton Juster, Diana Wynne-Jones, Margaret Mahy, Maurice Sendak, and William Steig – are far from free of social values. Occasionally a realistic writer makes a book with a fantasy element, such as Philippa Pearce's *Tom's Midnight Garden*, because it is the only way of saying what he or she wants to in that book.

It is sometimes thought that social critics are opposed to fantasy writing because it is escapist, favoring instead gritty realism. But it seems to me that children need *at least* two kinds of literature. They need books that portray people living the kinds of life they lead themselves (which is why domestic-realistic literature should reflect the widest possible range of lifestyles), and they need to be taken into other worlds as different as possible from

their own in order to stretch their imaginations, or rather, since children's imaginations are usually in better shape than adults', to keep their imaginations supple.

The fantasy element is both humorous and serious in C.S. Lewis's The Lion, the Witch and the Wardrobe.

ROLE REVERSAL

Feminists in particular have a bad name for taking traditional plot elements and just reversing the conventional sex roles. It is a useful method in a consciousness-raising group but very limited in what it can do in a children's story. I did a *little* of it myself in a story called *Beware, Princess!* which was written very much in the literary line of Jay Williams' *Practical Princess*. However, although my Princess Poppy is a resourceful and modern girl, caught in a society working on an older set of conventions, Prince Robin is no sissy either. When he turns up, the two youngsters have an adventure as equals, although Poppy does take the initiative. I hope there is a lot more that is unusual and amusing about *Beware, Princess!* than mere role change. But think how much fun it would be to write a modern version of *Robinson Crusoe* in which Crusoe was black and Friday white! However, as I have said elsewhere, and firmly believe, it is typical of the first wave of new writing to be concerned with redressing balances and swinging pendulums, so that role reversal will continue to be a strategy that is used in books where the discrimination in question is the subject of the book itself. This applies to *My Grandma Has Black Hair* as well as to *Girls Can Be Anything*, written several years before. Whenever you open up a new social area in children's books, it takes center stage. Later, when the pioneering phase is over, books can be about whatever else the writer wants, and unstereotyped characters will be in the background as well as in the limelight.

REWRITING TRADITIONAL STORIES

This is another technique practiced by some feminists. I would advise against it, for the simple reason that, as with role reversal, it is a single-idea technique that can soon become wearisome and predictable to read. It is really a kind of propaganda writing. The real problem about sex-stereotyping in traditional and fairy tales is an editorial one. As researcher and academic Heather Lyons showed in an excellent article, it was the late 19th- and early 20th- century editors who determined the shape of the classic fairy story collections so many of us grew up with. Some of the "lost" material with positive heroines, which Lyons has excavated, is published in Alison Lurie's *Clever Gretchen*.

THE INFLUENCE OF TELEVISION

The result of much of the television, movie and video viewing by children of the 80s is that they are much more sophisticated about plot devices like flashbacks, dream sequences and the intercutting of scenes. They are also used to being thrown in at the deep end of a story and picking up what's going on without long explanations from an anonymous narrator. Another feature they are accustomed to is quick-fire dialogue. On the whole this has had an admirable effect on children's literature. Not only is it shorter and tauter – it is less patronizing and tends to take the child reader into the story with it, without the intrusive narrator-voice making speeches or indulging in "purple" patches of description. This is one of many ways in which television works for and with books rather than against them.

MODELS FOR NEW WRITING

From all that has gone before, you can see that new writers wanting to get started need to think hard about how they relate to the children's literature of the past. It is natural, when you begin to write for children, to be influenced by the books that meant a lot to you in your own childhood. One publisher says that every so often she gets another manuscript which is really just Frances Hodgson Burnett's *The Secret Garden* in another guise. But while you are finding your own voice, it is as well to look at the work of some more recent writers than the ones you enjoyed as a child, or even the ones your own children liked best, if they have now grown up and left home, because children's books really have changed a lot.

For a start, long novels of 80,000 words plus are definitely a thing of the past, except for well-established authors with a large following or the odd freak title that makes it as a cult-book and bestseller. But do not use such books as a model! Books like *Watership Down* are published only once every decade or so. The average children's novel is now much shorter, even than it was in the 60s – even the longest ones for older readers are only 60,000 words or so at most. On the other hand, sequels, trilogies, quartets, even quintets, are as popular with older children as with their parents. Cynthia Voigt's stunning sequence of novels about the Tillerman family – *Homecoming, Dicey's Song, A Solitary Blue, The Runner* and *Come a Stranger* – have won her a sizable following on both sides of the Atlantic. Susan Cooper's *The Dark is Rising* books also have many admirers. Neither of these novel sequences is new writing, although the former is realism of extraordinary breadth and detail. Perhaps Rosa Guy's two trilogies about black teenagers in America – about Edith Jackson and Imamu Jones – are the best examples of new writing sustained over a large canvas.

The point about shorter novels is that a lot of leisurely – indeed even lazy – writing has gone. This is true of adult novels too. Although bestselling books are frequently fat blockbusters, most contemporary novels move at a faster pace than the ambling trot of Thackeray or the stately measure of Henry James.

Whether you are planning a full-length novel or a short picture book, spend time in the children's section of the library, getting to know the latest developments in the field, not with a view to copying, but in order to avoid redoing themes that have aready been done to death, and to saturate yourself in the best of contemporary writing and illustration. If that does not discourage you, you can start on the project you want with a surer sense of contemporary literary idioms.

CONCLUSION

If you have read this chapter carefully, as well as all the others in this book, you may by now feel that the whole business of writing for children is more difficult than it looks. It is! It's not a get-rich-quick business – only a handful of bestselling authors and illustrators make more than a modest living at it. Nor is it a matter of dashing off a bedtime story for loving children or grandchildren. Your books have to stand up against the competition of thousands of others for the attention of a vast readership of unknown children.

Nevertheless, if you still want to be a children's writer, it is no more difficult to be a "new writer" than any other kind. It is just adding one more discipline to the many required of the writer, the discipline of remaining aware that you are writing for children of many different kinds and colors, each one an individual as complex as any character you will create.

Chapter 4

Picture Books

The marketing area defined as "picture books" can cover almost anything produced for children from one to about seven years of age in which the illustration plays a significant part. It includes a bewildering diversity of types of books and styles of illustration and storytelling. A more accurate term might be "books for young children," and on closer inspection, we find that the majority of picture books *are* produced for use within a certain age range. The groups break down into one to three years, three to five years, and five to seven years, but there is also considerable interest in picture books among older children, enticed by those lovely illustrations.

HOOKED ON BOOKS: PUBLISHERS AND PICTURE BOOKS

For a publisher the commercial aspects of book publishing are paramount. The publisher's job is to manufacture and sell his product – which happens to be books. The author and/or illustrator's job is to ensure the quality of that product – publishers depend on your integrity to make that product the best one possible, for the most important consumers in the world – our children! Publishers have to consider their costs at all times: editing and in-house design costs, printing, warehousing, distribution and advertising costs. They live within a world sometimes dominated by concerns about co-productions with publishers in other countries, overseas sales, contract hassles, TV tie-ins, book awards (which can mean big sales increases), bestseller lists, book fairs at which they sell and buy rights to publish each other's books, and so on. To succeed within this world, they are always looking for new talent, and books which will *sell*. Yet publishers' commitment to picture books remains solid: why? Because despite a general slump in children's book sales, picture books have held their own.

Obviously very small children do not buy their own books, so picture book publishers have two major groups of book purchasers: parents and relatives; and teachers and librarians. Each group buys for subtly different reasons and has different expectations and requirements. Some of the changes that have occurred in picture books during the past 15 years have been the result of pressure from these consumers.

Basically, parents buy books to give pleasure, and apart from buying popular TV-series spin-offs, they often like to be guided in their choice by joining book clubs, reading lists of recommended books or subscribing to magazines which review new books. Supermarkets are, increasingly, selling cheap paperback and board books, and here children may well be making their own choices, so nice bright covers which attract them are needed!

Librarians simply want to see children reading and borrowing books, for pleasure. Teachers consider picture books largely for their usefulness to children learning to read, assuming an interaction between parent and child, or teacher and child, and accepting that pre-school nursery rhymes lay the foundations of literacy by giving children a sense of *pattern* in the sound of words.

Some teachers are teaching children to read entirely by using picture books, and devising their own annotated lists of books which follow firm guidelines: that the quality of the story must be such that it is "worth reading" (that is, worth the effort; that it bears being read aloud); that the story should encourage anticipation and prediction; that its external appearance is "eyecatching" and the illustrations "visually stimulating"; that it has clear, well-spaced print of a reasonable size, with lines comfortably spaced.

GETTING TO KNOW YOUR AUDIENCE

When you write and illustrate for children, there are two kinds of success: one is getting published and sold; the other is knowing that your book *really works* for children – and you are far more likely to achieve the latter if you know your audience. Contact with young children is essential if you are to become aware of their needs – the need for identific-

ation, for example: each child's need at some time or another to find a boy or girl exactly like himself or herself, in a book.

Then there are emotional and psychological needs: for reassurance; for relieving "bad" feelings through stories about wicked witches or naughty children; for reducing anxiety about, say, monsters under the bed or

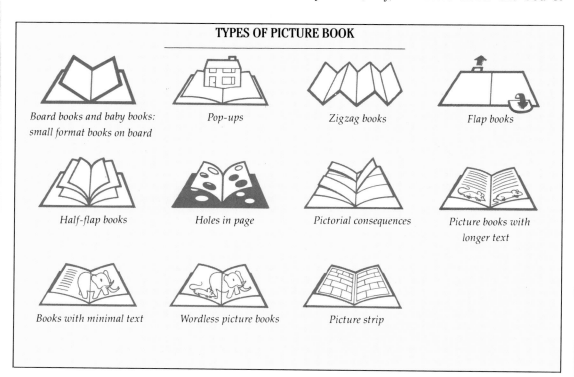

TYPES OF PICTURE BOOK

Board books and baby books: small format books on board

Pop-ups

Zigzag books

Flap books

Half-flap books

Holes in page

Pictorial consequences

Picture books with longer text

Books with minimal text

Wordless picture books

Picture strip

visits to the dentist. Children like to see *their* world reflected in books, and this can be accommodated in the illustrations in various ways: by use of contemporary detail, for instance, or by using a child's eye level, as if looking upward, or a bird's-eye view of interiors such as a child sees when up on its parent's shoulders looking down.

Children must be able to become involved in both pictures and text. Elaine Moss, critic, librarian and author, says: *"The picture books of the last 20 years are great, not because they confine the child's vision to the limits of the story, but because they invite the child in to roam about inside the picture."* [1]

Even in the less complicated toy books, children are actively involved in manipulating the movable parts and lifting the flaps, and their enjoyment of these books is part of playing, an aspect frequently mentioned in reviews. The context within which an editor may decide to publish an unsolicited manuscript is one in which he or she has to juggle a whole variety of considerations.

Thus commercial and business aspects, feedback from critics, reviewers, teachers, librarians, pressure groups, parents and children will all affect the outcome. If you are aware of this and plan accordingly, you will increase your chances of publication.

TYPES OF PICTURE BOOK

With most picture books, production decisions determine the form and format, and vice versa. A book with lots of lift-up flaps will need to be printed on stiff cardboard, so it will need a stout binding and be quite thick: such a book will probably have a short text, and fall into the category of "toy books." A longish folk tale would be unlikely to lend itself to such a format. Stories and story lines range from very slight to extremely complex and subtle, providing something for children's needs at every stage of their competence, sophistication, understanding, and increasing knowledge of narrative.

Illustrations can have human or animal characters; be set in city, town or country, today, last century, in nursery-rhyme land or middle-European "folk-tale" land; and range in treatment from ultra-simplified outlines (such as Virginia Lee Burton) to highly elaborate realism or detailed fantasy (Edna Miller).

1: *The Audience for Children's Books.* Elaine Moss. Pub. The National Book League (now Book Trust), 1979.

ALPHABET BOOKS AND COUNTING BOOKS

Always among the most steadily popular of all picture books, ABCs sell widely today. Authors and illustrators find ingenious new ways of presenting the alphabet, while traditional ABCs are reissued and still largely successful. Alphabet books can range from the extremely simple format of Dick Bruna – one letter and one schematic object per spread – to the brief nonsense rhymes explaining each letter in Fritz Eichenberg's *Ape in a Cape*.

There are numerical counterparts to alphabet books: many children will have a counting book among their earliest possessions. As the numbers rarely go above 10, counting books can be tricky to fit into the usual picture-book paginations of 24 or 32 pages. Publishers have produced some baby board books of only 16 pages. Again, as with ABCs, counting books range from the extremely simple to the subtly complex, in which the pictures contain not only the specified number of objects, but tell their own story: such as Sandra Boynton's *Hippos go Berserk*.

Below *Brian Wildsmith's* ABC *opened up a new world to illustrators.* **Right** *Dick Bruna's crisp line and flat colors first made baby books popular in the 60s.* **Below right** *Rosalinda Kightley's* The Little Red Car. **Far Left** *The lovable* Spot *by Eric Hill.*

Board books and baby books

Board books are literally books that are printed on paper, then laminated onto stout, childproof board, usually small enough for toddlers' hands to hold with ease. Publishers have been producing many other books in this very small size, often with a stout cover: these are referred to as "baby books," and both types are usually stocked together. Intended for very young children and babies, they tend to be of simple format (for example, *Bunnykins ABC*), often consisting of pictures of everyday objects and one or two words of text per page. Occasionally, real stories are published in this tiny size, such as *Edwin's Adventures* by Mary Chell with illustrations by Tamasin Cole.

The little red car was out for a drive. Beep, beep!

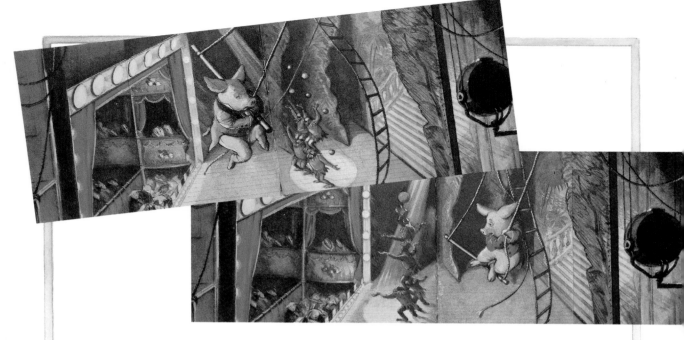

Toy books

Toy books are produced in a variety of formats throughout the picture book age range. *Pop-ups* have been with us since the 19th century and are so well known as to need no description. The paper engineering required is quite complicated, so they are not for the amateur, unlike *zigzag* books, a form of board book which can open out to make a frieze and be used for alphabet or counting books. Recently, a highly successful form of toy book has been the kind where the illustration contains a *glued-on flap* for the child to lift up, revealing the picture concealed underneath.

Foldaways have also enjoyed a revival late-ly: in this, the illustration is folded back on itself to conceal a part of the picture which, when opened out, renders the image comic or ludi-

Above *John Goodall's ingeniously simple half-flap wordless picture book evokes a lost world of the past.* **Left** *Whose Footprints? by Jean Baylis and Doreen Smith cleverly uses both the frieze and the half-flap technique to introduce toddlers to the concept of an animal and its footprints — with a surprise under each flap.*

Right *The Elephant and the Bad Baby by Elfrida Vipont, illustrated by Raymond Briggs.*

crous. (It's fun for children to make their own.) John Goodall has made the *half-flap* wordless picture book entirely his own: bound into the center of each spread is a half-page which overlaps within the main illustration, and changes the content of the picture, when turned over, to further the narrative sequence. Some books are cut in half or thirds horizontally to make a form of *pictorial consequences* and some books have *holes cut in the pages* which reveal part of the next page. What toy books have in common is an element of surprise, and they engage the child in the book as a form of play. (See also *Fad Books*, page 114.)

Nursery rhymes, folk and fairy tales

There is perpetual demand from parents and playgroups for collections of nursery rhymes and traditional stories. They lend themselves to a picture-book treatment very well; they do not date, and they sell steadily for a long time. Raymond Briggs' *Mother Goose* and *Fairy Tale Treasury* are still going strong after over 20 years.

MANY WORDS, FEW WORDS, NO WORDS AND PICTURE STRIP

The majority of picture books have a text of between 200 and 1,000 words. This means that larger areas of text have to be a smaller type size in the layout, and it is usually assumed these will be suitable for slightly older children. This is still a very small number of words with which to tell a story, and each one must "pay its way," giving a picture-book text many of the qualities of a poem. This poetic feel is often reflected in the form of the story, such as the cumulative tale; for example, *The Elephant and the Bad Baby* by Elfrida Vipont, illustrated by Raymond Briggs. It is a classic tale of the baby "who never once said please" until more and more people run after him and the elephant. Many texts use a rhythmical repetition of words or phrases, such as *My Cat likes to Hide in Boxes* by Eve Sutton or *The Doorbell Rang* by Pat Hutchins, and echo the word patterns with lots of visual patterns. And, of course, some stories are told entirely in verse.

Books with minimal text

One picture is worth a thousand words . . . . Picture book authors have taken this maxim to heart to produce some 20th-century classics. Picture books with minimal text work in a variety of ways by being read, looked at, and enjoyed on many levels simultaneously.

The illustrations can show actions or events which extend beyond the narrative, so that the reader knows something the hero or heroine of the book does not – in the same way that the audience at a Punch-and-Judy type of children's show can see a crocodile or wolf creeping up behind the oblivious hero; (*Rosie's Walk* by Pat Hutchins is a good example). The picture can show a wider social context than the words convey, enabling a child to relate to the world contained inside the pictures, by

picture books, such as *Each Peach Pear Plum* by Allan and Janet Ahlberg, draw on the reader's knowledge of other stories and nursery rhymes to enrich the text and add context to pictorial detail.

Wordless picture books and picture strip

Invariably the work of author/illustrators, wordless picture books have to be devised by very visually-minded writers, and picture strips are strictly for the professional illustrator. Many picture books have spreads without text, which extend the sense of time as the reader experiences the book. The wordless picture book is

scrutinizing and becoming involved in the details. In *Having a Picnic* by Sarah Garland, the words are few and simple, but the pictures show us mommy struggling single-handed on a windy day in a wintry city park.

The text can be reduced to a minimum if the pictures are "telling most of the story." This reverses the usual order of importance of words over pictures, and the text gains a limpid poetic clarity for the sound of the words. Some

an extension of this device and works by depending on the reader's knowledge of narrative: that is, by assuming that the child reading it has already learned what to expect from stories, and will project a story onto the sequence of illustrations, or deduce a story from details and changes within the pictures.

Picture strip can be used to compress a lot of information and story together and can also be used to vary layout and give a sense of expansion to a delightfully light tale such as *Could be Worse.*

Left *The award-winning* Each Peach Pear Plum *by Janet and Allan Ahlberg uses a simple nursery rhyme text form with an accompanying illustration of great complexity and visual interest — a scene of hidden clues for a child to endlessly explore.* **Above** *Philippe Dupasquier uses the four seasons as the basis for a rich wordless tale* Our House on the Hill. *Raymond Briggs also uses wordless strips for his incomparable* The Snowman (**right**).

MARRYING PICTURES AND TEXT

A picture-book text leaves the pictures to do most of the work, as the example here shows. The words themselves leave a lot unsaid but when married to the rough thumbnail sketches a humorous story begins to unfold. The example shows the opening spreads from a 24-page picture book.

Mom and Dad love Audrey.

Even though Audrey is sometimes naughty.

Even though Audrey is sometimes rude.

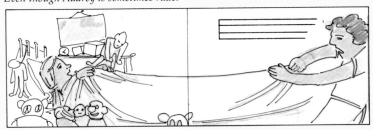

Even though Audrey won't get up in the morning.

And won't go to bed at night.

WRITING A PICTURE-BOOK TEXT

A quick browse in any bookstore or public library will show you that most picture books are either 24 or 32 pages long – including the title page and copyright page – and baby board books usually have 16 pages. You will see that books are always produced in multiples of eight pages. The majority of first-time picture-book writers produce a longish first draft, up to 1,000 words or more, which will mean a 32-page book, if the type is to be reasonably large. Most texts benefit from pruning: cutting your text down makes for a richer, denser narrative with no superfluous padding. A picture book is *not* a short story: a short story stands on its own and does not necessarily need illustration; it is a complete artistic creation. A picture-book text leaves a lot unsaid; it makes room for the pictures to tell the story too and ought to sound odd and half-naked on its own – it is not *meant* to be read without its pictures!

The writer must work out all the details of character and sequence of events, and decide which are to be written about and which are to go in the pictures. This can be difficult for people who don't have a strong visual imagination. Sometimes a writer has a good idea but finds it difficult to develop that idea into a full story; or the story may work out well and its pictures follow naturally, but be awkward to fit into a 32-page picture-book length. These are problems which your editor and illustrator can help with.

Some of the very best picture books have as their starting point a straightforward observation of some aspects of a child's daily life. Children have two worlds, both equally "real" to them: the activities and events which happen to them outwardly and the inner thoughts and feelings they have about those events and the important people in their lives, such as their parents, brothers, sisters and teachers. Picture books can be about both the "external" and "internal" realities of a child's world, but the internal realities are difficult to illustrate and need to have a tangible external manifestation.

If, for instance, your book is partly about jealousy, which looms large in any childhood with siblings in it, as every parent knows, how is that to be depicted? The writer needs not to state it explicitly, but to have an event and illustrations that outwardly reflect the inner feeling.

THINGS TO WATCH OUT FOR IN YOUR WRITING

- *Dialogue* Too much dialogue is tedious to read aloud and dull to illustrate because there is no action. Consider putting dialogue into your prospective illustrations in the form of speech balloons – a favorite device used by Maurice Sendak and Edward Ardizzone.

- *Cultural differences* Certain details may cause problems for the illustrator when co-publishing and overseas sales are considered: food varies so much from country to country; vehicles drive on different sides of the road; typical pets, landscapes, buildings and so on vary. Watch out for these details in your writing and planning.

- *Rhyming verse* Many editors have reservations about stories written in verse because of a feeling that verse is often the resort of people who cannot handle prose; the same story in prose may be revealed as very flat and banal. At the very simple level of picture book text, verse tends to trivialize the story by making it sound humorous and thus giving it overtones of slightness. For the illustrator, a formal verse structure is bound to be reflected in a formalized layout, which will need to be varied by ingenious means if the book is not to look too repetitive.

THE AUTHOR/ILLUSTRATOR'S PICTURE-BOOK

A natural illustrator sees "pictures in the head" when reading a story, and some writers have a strong visual sense and are able to draw pictures to their own texts. More usually, after some years' experience, many picture-book illustrators find it natural to have ideas for stories, particularly after they have had children of their own. The author/illustrator is the ideal picture-book producer, because the pictures will be exactly as the writer envisioned them, and words and pictures should be perfectly blended. An author/illustrator is unlikely to produce a picture book in two completely separate stages – first the words, then the pictures – he will probably have instinctive feelings about illustrations right from the first moment of having the idea and is likely to be working out the story and planning pictures simultaneously. But at some point, the text has to be written out separately for presentation in manuscript form to the prospective publishers; and the pictures have to be worked out in their layout, in the same way an illustrator works out a picture book when interpreting another writer's text.

How to go about it

Take your time over planning: let the book grow. After that initial flash of inspiration, give your book several months to take shape. You must find that core of creativity inside yourself to polish a good idea into a full-fledged artifact. Ponder it; put your storyboard or flat-plan up on the wall and live with it for a while; and make changes to it as the ideas hit you. If you are working all day at another job this will have to happen anyway, and you will be making space for your book in your spare time. Don't worry, this is how a book would naturally happen. Even if you actually wrote it all down in one weekend, the story has probably been germinating inside you for months! In any case, if you wish to succeed in a picture-book career, you will have to acquire patience and self-discipline if you don't have them

already, and also the ability to switch off from all other distractions and concentrate totally on your book. So in some ways, having to work at your book part-time is good training. Your working methods should be similar to those of the interpretive illustrator (see *Making a Book*, page 80).

Try your story at both 24- and 32-page lengths. Making a dummy reveals exactly where the story does not work and also suggests what structural changes need to be made. It is surprising how often the tiny thumbnail sketches on the manuscript or pictures in the dummy do form the basis of the eventual page. If your book is accepted, you can expect help from your editor and designer, but an unsolicited book stands a much better chance of success if it is accompanied by a dummy in which the main details have been fully sorted out and it can be seen that the whole book "works."

Submitting an unsolicited picture book

Prepare a typed, double-spaced manuscript, numbered according to your proposed pagination – either 24 pages or 32 pages, with the text beginning on pages 3 or 5 – accompanied by a complete dummy of text and sketchy, but reasonably clear, pictures to give an idea of how you see the book, plus a couple of finished specimen illustrations – with no text on them – to indicate your style and proficiency. (You won't know page dimensions at this stage, and it is unlikely that you will use these illustrations, so don't do more than two.) Keep a photocopy of *everything*; not only in case of loss but also so that you have your copy to refer to during correspondence and telephone discussions.

Choose a publisher by looking at picture books and select someone who seems to publish your kind of book; addresses are printed on the copyright page; address your manuscript to the Children's Editor. If you have not heard from them after a month, telephone to find out what is happening. Some publishers receive up to a thousand unsolicited children's book proposals each year, and will accept maybe two percent of them, so be *very very* polite: editors are extremely busy, and unsolicited books do not take priority. On the other hand, they are always looking for new talent and new books that are good and *will* sell, so do not jeopardize your chances by hassling them or arguing.

BEING AWARE...

The author/illustrator becomes deeply aware of how the pictures tell the story – by detail, by changes of scene from one page to the next, by depiction of action, by facial expressions – and anyone who has read picture books with children will know how keenly they scan the pictures to pick up that information and build it into the story. In a way, you need to draw, as it were, from inside a child's mind: you need to be imaginatively in touch with seeing things as children see them. Be aware, too, of the variety of ways of visualizing available to you: consider the pictorial devices that children like and use in their own drawings, such as speech balloons, bits of picture strip, the occasional cross section, and so on.

You have a lot of choices available as to styles and treatment. You can use animals or human characters; your settings can be city, town, rural or domestic interiors; present-day or long-ago; photo-realistic or stylized and simplified; full of pattern and elaborate detail, or quietly understated. Every choice will give your pictures a different look and "tone"; you have to decide which one you want your book to have.

Beginners often have a limited style: experience and/or training develops illustrators' capacity to be flexible and to vary their personal style. Most beginners' faults are easy to remedy – they often draw lines too thin for reproduction; do not leave enough room for the text; do not make bleed areas sufficiently wide; write words and names inside the picture in color – words should be in black only or vague and unreadable, because of translation considerations for foreign-language editions. Try to know your own faults, such as habitually drawing children who look too large and old to be toddlers, or who look too thin, too tall, too short, too large-headed for child-appeal.

It *is* difficult to accommodate your illustrations to what you may know about children's likes and dislikes, so if you show your work-in-progress to a toddler, don't be perturbed by individual idiosyncrasies. Certain perceptual difficulties obviously have to be taken into account, which is why some picture books are regarded as suitable for older children. Testing books is the responsibility of the publisher, who may well arrange to have your roughs shown to a nursery school, just to obtain some feedback. This is really only important for books aimed primarily at the education market or for those intended to be informational rather than fictional. As Jill Bennett says: "*In the end, a book has no meaning other than what is created by its maker and an individual reader and this will always be personal.*"[2]

Lovely detailed illustration in Alan Baker's Benjamin's Portrait *makes it a favorite with three to seven year olds.*

2: *Learning to Read with Picture Books.* Pub. Thimble Press, 1985.

INTERPRETING A PICTURE-BOOK TEXT

An amateur, untrained would-be illustrator is not going to be commissioned to illustrate picture books; there is too much competition. But untrained illustrators *can* break into picture-book publishing by writing their own.

- You need to be sure you have been properly briefed, especially when amplifying a minimal text. The author should have put a lot of thought into the proposed illustrations before you see the manuscript; and the author is responsible for the strength of the story – no amount of illustration can disguise a weak, flat story.

- If you are wondering whether you are able to illustrate picture books, consider re-illustrating one of the classic children's stories to get the feel of it.

- Cultivate studio discipline and schedule your time to meet deadlines; remember those print and reproduction considerations; stick to the specifications; ask your editor if you have queries.

Choosing your style and treatment
Your style and treatment will affect how your pictures function, and will tend to determine the age level the book is pitched at. You have a range of styles to choose from, and you must select the one that is appropriate for the "tone" of the book. Styles do different things – they can be sentimental or tough; hard or fluffy; humorous, serious or plain factual; fast and furious, drawn with fierce rapid energy; or neat and careful, drawn with architectural accuracy – the possibilities are infinite; the applications, specific. For example, the style and treatment used by Eric Hill for his "Spot" books is simplified but humorous, with solid outlines blocked in within flat color and minimal detail. This style, which can convey action, simple settings, a short sequence of events and a moderate emotional range, makes it appropriate for young children.

Vary your layout
One large illustration across each spread with the text at the top, looks quite monotonous after 30 pages. So don't forget about all the pictorial innovations mentioned previously: picture strips; pictures within pictures as "thought" balloons or "meanwhiles" (as used in *What did you do in the Holidays?*); eccentrically shaped pictures – they do not have to be square or rectangular or oval – or the use of an unexpected setting.

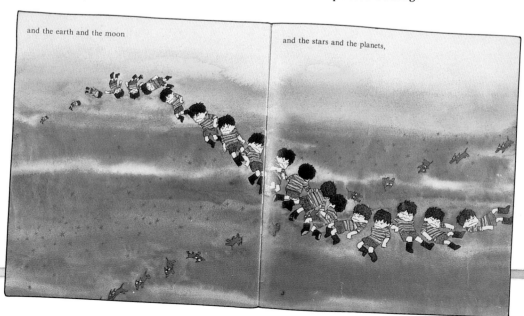
and the earth and the moon

and the stars and the planets,

Using animals

Illustrating with animals as characters effects a subtle change in how the reader responds. It can be very useful for stories dealing with diffuse feelings of the kind that children have all the time but cannot describe as such and that would be too harsh to illustrate in a realistic style with children. Russell Hoban's "Frances" stories and Maurice Sendak's bears and alligators for Else Holmelund Minarik are brilliant examples of animals used in this way.

Animals can also be used when the main characters are adult but childish and you want reader identification. In the text for *Forget-Me-Not* the author envisioned a boy who travels alone to the beach. For the events in the story to be feasible, this character could only be an adult; so, to retain child interest, he was turned into a kindly lion and the whole book was illustrated with anthropomorphic lions.

Far left Satoshi Kitamura uses a bold *"fantastic" approach to the design of the spreads in* Angry Arthur — *here the power of the child's personality is strikingly portrayed.* **Left** *Michael Foreman, a master of technique, is able to bend his imagination around any problem. In* Private Zoo — *written by Georgess McHargue — he creates an inspired visual double-take on each spread.*

BEING INFORMED

For anyone hoping to make a career in children's books, it is a great help to be well informed: to *look* at children's books; to *be* with children; to *read* the relevant literature; or all three! Any parents of young children will inevitably find themselves looking at current picture books in stores and libraries, and will soon notice which ones appeal and also how individual are children's choices. (It is no coincidence that many picture-book authors and artists came to it after having children for the first time.) There are some sound reasons for being well informed about picture books in particular:

- There is such an abundance of new ones that it is important that you do not accidentally duplicate a book that has already been "done" and thus have your idea rejected.

- It is worthwhile to be informed about current taste in picture books, so you can see which publisher tends to publish which kind of books, and submit your (unsolicited) manuscript to the most likely one.

- It is always better to be on the wavelength of young children today, to avoid nostalgia and harking back to your own childhood: nothing dates a book so much as anachronistic details, and publishers know that children spurn books which feel to them "out of date."

Chapter 5

Illustration – Building a Career in Children's Books

The illustration of children's books – in both line and full color – provides the perfect opportunity for joining together the work of two vivid imaginations to form a superb whole. To many publishers – and some authors and artists – illustrations are there simply to sell books, to make them more attractive to the eye, to encourage customers to pick them up and perhaps on impulse to take them home because they are bright and cheerful.

ILLUSTRATION FOR CHILDREN'S BOOKS: PERFECT MARRIAGE OR ARMED TRUCE?

Making it easier to understand the story and breaking up daunting pages of solid text with harmonious arrangements of text with the open or detailed line of engravings and wood cuts has for centuries been the understood role of illustrators. But so much more can be achieved and often was in the great partnerships of the past. Here is the artist Hilda van Stockum, writing wittily and perceptively on the partnership of Dickens and Cruikshank:

" . . . the engravings in Dickens . . . are a perfect example of the art of illustrating. They tell the story you're reading, not some other story the artist prefers. One even suspects the illustrator read the book, perhaps more than once. The people in the pictures are the same as in the book, with some details added which the author forgot to mention, and the pictures are placed where and when you expect them, at satisfying climaxes and dramatic moments, taking care of situations the author had to leave in a hurry . . . He can't develop an intricate plot and bring it to an exciting explosion with everything happening at once unless he leaves some things to look after themselves. It is at those moments, when the author has to drop everything to rush after his story, that the illustrator must rise to the occasion and put the baby to bed, warm the soup, sweep the floor and show that the rest of the world is going on as usual." [1]

Thus the author needs the illustrator to tell the story in a parallel manner, while the artist needs the author to provide a strong and vigorous plot as the stimulus to his or her imagination. *But* the author is then owed a certain debt of loyalty – a faithfulness to the mood and spirit of the narrative. When required to "put the baby to bed," the illustrator must not decide that it would be altogether more fun for the baby if he were to take it to the races

---

1: from "The Horn Book Magazine" quoted in *The Illustrator's Note Book*, Ed Lee Kingman, Boston, 1978.

George Cruikshank and Charles Dickens became one of the first fruitful partnerships in 19th-century English literature. Cruikshank's vigorous warts-and-all style perfectly captured both the humor and the humanity of many of Dickens' most absurd characters. In Sketches by Boz *he turns his sharp eye and sharper pen loose on the characters of Victorian London.*

instead. A fine illustrator doing inappropriate illustrations as a showcase for his own visual pyrotechnics for an equally fine author's text is a waste of time, effort and money.

Illustrations need to be *part* of a story, fleshing out characters the author has merely sketched: the words providing clues to their personalities while the pictures give them a physical reality in their proper background and setting. In ideal combinations, the verbal and visual aspects complement and strengthen one another, alerting the reader with a chilling phrase or a single shadowed stroke to a change in the mood or fortunes of the character. True illustrators will handle the text with intelligence, clarity and faithfulness while adding to it an indefinable "something" from their own per-

sonalities. They will also project themselves forward to touch the mind of the child who will read the words and dream over the pictures. The child who looks and looks, can – unlike a constantly distracted adult – give himself up to the concentrated contemplation of an illustration, looking into its every corner for "happenings" and the details of an imaginary world.

Some illustrators try to curry favor with children by pretending to "see things like a child" by doing childlike or childish drawings. But a child doesn't see the world in simplified images filled with stick people. A child's "vision" of the world is probably clearer, sharper and more uncluttered with preconception than that of the adult illustrator. It is only the technical skill which children lack when they try to

Shirley Hughes, the creator of numerous unforgettable children, has given us a true heroine in her illustrations for Dorothy Edwards' My Naughty Little Sister.

portray their world in its full complexity, and children will quickly dismiss the poor efforts of the illustrators who copy *them*. The only person who can draw like a child . . . is a child. True simplicity, on the other hand, is the ability to select and edit, to see and know and *choose* what to include and what to exclude. It is the result of great skill and sophistication and is the opposite of a naive or "childlike" view, which includes everything and excludes nothing. Simplicity comes later – and produces a Chinese bowl or a Beethoven quartet.

Meanwhile there are books to look at with words and pictures to fill every inch of a child's imagination – pictures to return to again and again. Shirley Hughes, one of today's most accomplished and popular illustrators, has described the illustrator's role perfectly:

"Like an actor (or rather a whole company of actors, scene designers and director in one), the illustrator starts with a text which springs from somebody else's imagination. He must immerse himself in it and work his way out intuitively before, summoning all his powers of research and imagination, he uses it as a springboard from which to jump. The idea is to give the author and publisher not what they want, but what they never dreamed they could have."[2]

2: from "A Telling Line" by Shirley Hughes, *Illustrators 33*, London, 1980.

PRESENTING YOURSELF

"Hello, is that the Art Director? I'm an illustrator…" These are the opening lines of countless telephone conversations I've had over the years. How do I *know* you're an illustrator? More important, how do *you* know you're an illustrator and not just a dabbler, who has always been good at drawing, but isn't quite sure about delivering it by next Tuesday – *"You know – er – the inspiration might not come…"* More illustrators' careers have failed to start or quickly foundered, after a few poorly handled, badly organized and late delivered jobs, because of a lack of the right temperament than lack of talent. You think that won't happen to you? Good!

Now read on…

Art directors, art editors and children's book editors who commission illustration always try to make some time in every busy week to see the portfolios of new artists. It is an essential part of the job they do – and often one of its pleasures. But, because the time taken to look thoroughly and sympathetically through several folios a week is time carefully saved from other, more pressing, duties, it's up to the visiting illustrators to make that time as productive as possible.

Over the past 20-odd years I've seen thousands of folios from artists of all kinds: students, newly-minted graduates, untrained self-taught geniuses, busy working professionals and ladies up from the country who are hoping that the drawings they do for their grandchildren can earn them some money. Successful book illustrators have come from *all* of these groups – and not just because of a rare or special talent. The best are also the most well organized and well supported (and part of *that* is recognizing when an agent can best act for them, finding such an agent and letting the agent get on with the "business" of their lives while *they* get on with the books!). They are also the most down-to-earth about money matters, seeking good advice and taking it. Doesn't sound very "artistic", does it?

The myth of the "artist as dreamer" is just that – a myth. The illustrators who work, *get* work; those who dream continue to have plenty of time for this pleasant, but notoriously uncommercial, occupation.

It's also a truism that the artist any art director really *wants* for a particular job is already busy. So art directors may turn to the week's rush of new illlustrators, hoping to find the perfect person to take on the job. The vast majority of those showing their folios around publishing houses and ad agencies are newly graduated students with virtually no printed work to show and those with one or two years of experience whose folios are a mixture of student work and professional, printed work. The good ones will soon have specimens showing an ever-widening range of work carried out as commissions for books or magazines. The more printed work you have the better. It indicates that: a) your student or amateur specimens were good enough to interest a client who then commissioned you to do a job; b) you were able to carry out that job successfully and in the agreed manner; c) you understood enough about working for reproduction to create an illustration (or several!) which printed well and you were proud enough of to include as a specimen in your folio; and d) that your work does look attractive when translated from a hand-created "original" into a mechanically reproduced "duplicate-object." If all this comes across in a quick flip through a well-presented folio, then you are on your way. For the novice, however, some advice may be helpful.

Doing the rounds

If you are coming into the city from a fairly long distance and can give several weeks' notice of your planned visit, then a letter to the publishing houses your hope to see is appropriate. If you don't get a reply from one or two, then follow up your letter with a telephone call. Art directors are notoriously lax about answering casual inquiries for appointments – there never seems to be enough time! A reply *might* be more forthcoming if you enclose a self-addressed postcard with *Yes/No*, along with date and time choices, ready for the quick tick of a secretary's pen after she's checked the diary. But if you can, it's best to call for an appointment. Always get the name of the person you want to see – the switchboard will help you. You will want either the art director or art editor, or, in firms where individual editors commission illustrations for their own lists, the children's editor dealing with the kind of books you want to do. It is sometimes tricky but important – in small firms one person may handle all the commissioning, while in a larger firm, with many imprints, there will be several. Note the name (or names) on your own list of publishing houses whose

work you like – or in your copy of *Writer's Market* or the *L.M.P.* (see *Appendix*, page 138).

Knowing *who* to contact is essential, and that first visit is less nerve-racking if you've actually spoken beforehand to the person you will meet. Learning to *spell* those names is equally important. I could paper the wall with the variations on my own name that have graced envelopes over the years – it makes a poor first impression if someone doesn't take the trouble to get it right.

Speak to the right person or his or her secretary and make an appointment, giving as much information about the kind of work you do and any previous experience, if they ask. If a publisher thinks you may be someone whose work they can use, you'll get an appointment. The telephone questions are really to weed out people whose work is really *not* suitable for children's books.

The first house you call may give you a date several weeks ahead – very few people can drop everything in reply to one of those "I'm-in-town-for-the-day-and-would-like-to-show-you-my-work" calls. Once you have the first appointment, then ring other houses and set up a series for that day or that week.

Check the addresses against a city plan and arrange to see houses in one area in the morning (or on Monday . . .) and those in another part of town in the afternoon (or on Tuesday), and so on.

Give yourself a comfortable lunch break and leave at least half an hour between each appointment – even if your next "port of call" is only a few streets away – just in case your previous meeting runs on longer than planned. There may be several reasons for this: the person you've come to see may be delayed with a meeting, a crisis or a "late lunch"; if it's a large company, there may be several people who will want to look at your folio; or – and this does happen – the client may like your work and think you might be *just* the person to illustrate a manuscript which is due in this week. (And, as you're in the office, it's sensible to run over the details of a proposed sample illustration there and then . . . .) But, even without the heady excitement of a real job arising out of one of your interviews, you'll find that you will welcome the break – to freshen up, or have a cup of coffee and then travel calmly to the next address. *Don't* arrive 15 minutes late, flustered and with your portfolio in a muddle ready to drop at the feet of the next art director. Publishers are among the nicest people you'll meet and work for in the illustration world, but they will be more impressed with you – and your work – if you arrive at each appointment *looking as if it were the first of the day.*

I "did the rounds" during a bitter Boston February in the mid-1960s, and found an overwhelmingly helpful, warm and enthusiastic response from everyone I saw, especially publishers – only partly attributable to the fact that it was "off-season" for art students. The stormier the weather became, the more comfortable armchairs, cups of coffee and recommendations to opposite numbers in other houses were pressed upon me. The disconcerting result of all this unexpected largesse was that, by the end of the week, I positively loathed the work in my folio and longed to find that, for my next appointment, several new specimens had tucked themselves between those handy plastic sleeves.

To make myself feel that it was different each time, I found that an extra few minutes spent in the ladies' room of the ad agency or publishing house I'd just visited was enough to rearrange the order of all the specimens. When I next opened it an hour later, I was greeted with a fresh image and, therefore, felt a little less jaded. Of course, to each client it *was* new – my shuffling trick wasn't for their benefit but for my own. If you don't feel enthusiasm for what you're doing (not self-satisfaction, just enthusiasm) when you start, how can you expect a stranger, however sympathetic, to feel any?

From then on I surreptitiously shuffled all day and often substituted different pieces each evening. This simple trick of "self-delusion" was enough of a morale booster, and by the end of that cold and snowy February, I had my first job – as an art editor!

A postscript

When you make an appointment – keep it! On the right day of the right week and on time. If you can't make it because of illness, a domestic crisis, a rushed deadline on a job or general funk – call and cancel it. When you do keep the appointment, remember that the people you want to see are *always* too busy to see you, so make them glad that they took the time out of a hectic day to do so. Courtesy counts, in getting the job, fulfilling the commission and going on to more work for a satisfied client. It's one of the hallmarks of being a professional.

PREPARING THE FOLIO

What you bring when presenting yourself and how you bring it are vital. Treat yourself to a comprehensive browse around big bookstores and, if possible, a specialist children's bookstore. Work-hunting young illustrators invariably say that they are interested in children's books but often have no idea what they mean by that. Only a few young illustrators actually look at – let alone read – children's books for their own pleasure. You need to know what is being published by whom! What are the current trends, if any, in both text and illustrations? Do you see a lot of strong, clear lines filled in with bright, flat color *à la* Dick Bruna or Eric Hill, or is publishing going through another wave of nostalgia with Noddy and Flower Fairies on every rack? Are the picture-book spinners filled with smiling-faced steam engines or small woodland animals in sprigged muslin dresses? Are space technology and SF in or out? Does everything have holes in it, pop up, or turn into a menacing robot? Are you looking at the book-of-the-toy-of-the-TV-series or the toy-of-the-TV-series-of-the-book? In fact, the present children's book field seems to encompass past, present and future with a very wide range of illustration styles which have found favor with children of all ages. It is a good climate for illustrators.

Every publishing house has its own feel or flavor, and a look through bookstores and publishers' catalogs will give some clue to this. The illustration needs of today's publishers range from "classic" black and white line drawings for hardback novels, to joke, puzzle and story-book illustrations for paperbacks, through every conceivable combination of line and full color for fiction, nonfiction and picture books, to those special novelty toy-books that require elaborate paper-engineering and design skills. The publishing philosophy of any given house may be one imposed by a clear-cut marketing strategy or one that has grown up around the style of one particular charismatic editor. If you understand the differences between houses,

you can then have specimens to show that indicate that you *have* taken the time and the trouble to acquaint yourself with the list of each publisher you visit. This makes a good first impression and shows that you are a discriminating would-be professional who has taken more trouble than the average seeker-of-work.

Some portfolios are a joy to leaf through: the specimens are chosen with care, and wit, to show the work that best displays skills in *figure drawing, character, setting and narrative* – all essentials for children's book illustration. Twenty interchangeable presentation drawings of new-model cars airbrushed to glowing perfection may well be *exactly* the thing to show to the art buyer of an advertising agency that has just landed a major account with Ford or Jaguar, but they are of negligible interest to a hard-pressed art editor with three joke books, four "fighting fantasy" game books and a huge series of full-color storybooks to produce against an impossible deadline. Professionalism counts in the relationship of publisher and illustrator, and the publisher, in agreeing to take a personal look at the portfolio (rather than

DOING THE ROUNDS PREPARED

SELECT WITH CARE.

I'LL LEAVE THIS ONE OUT!

the "please-leave-it-and-we'll-let-you-know" approach) will expect in return that the illustrator will have made him- or herself aware of *who* the client is and what business it is in.

Once you have organized a day – or several days – of visits and made a note of what each publisher specializes in, then you can plan the contents of your folio. Spread everything out on the floor and walk slowly around it. Ask friends and family to help you to choose the most effective pieces – and, remember, be RUTHLESS. Throw out those liquid-eyed pussy-cats, the Christmas cards you designed for Auntie Vi a year ago, most of the life-class nudes on brown paper heightened with white conté, *every* silkscreen print of Elvis Presley or Marilyn Monroe, all but the *best* of those illustrations done in the current fashionable style – be it Bayley or Burningham – and, when you've done that, I hope that most of what is left is really *you*. Choose a dozen (yes, just 12) pieces, including drawings from life, not from photographs, of children and adults in motion, portrait sketches, observational drawings, costumes and period detail, landscape/townscape and at least one board with several small drawings or paintings illustrating a given text and showing narrative development. If this last is an example of published work, include the rough dummy or storyboard as well. This is an excellent way to show how you plan a job. If covers are a special interest, include the two or three best examples. Include nothing that doesn't stand on its own. If you find yourself needing to provide long-winded explanations for every specimen you show, those specimens have failed as illustrations and shouldn't be in your portfolio. Good illustration communicates – it doesn't need a running commentary!

When you've done all the agonizing and have a selection worthy of your taste and talent, consider how best to carry it impressively from place to place. Leave behind the tatty shopping bags, the cardboard rolls of posters and prints – they are hard to extract, difficult to show flat and impossible to replace in a hurry – and that old box of moody black and white photographs with their curling edges. Buy, or make, a small, easily handled folio. Leather ones are expensive and heavy to carry, and there are now several lightweight alternatives in molded plastic or laminated cardboard. They come in attractive colors which can be further personalized.

If you carry too much, you'll be flustered

and exhausted by dragging this cumbersome burden with you. Publishers all work in paper-piled offices of cell-like dimensions. Flat surfaces are invariably filled with valuable work-in-progress, and there just isn't room for your giant string-tied folio bulging with endless variations on similar themes. I've viewed hundreds of folios kneeling on the floor with artists perched somewhere just out of range – because there was not enough room for artist and folio in a small crowded office. Books are produced in a wide variety of formats, but none is *ever* as large as the average student portfolio. Look at children's books and think again – the majority of them range in size from a minimum of 7 x 4in for standard paperbacks to a maximum of 12 x 9in for the largest hardback picture books. Only a few books are produced in a larger format.

For color work the most effective way to show a wide range of pieces is with plastic pocket-sheets of 35mm transparencies. Most offices you visit will have a light box or slide viewer as part of their standard equipment, but you can also carry a small slide viewer with you – having dispensed with the weight of your giant-size folio, you'll have plenty of room for a few "high tech" extras.

Unencumbered, and taking only your best work, you will feel more confident and will present yourself better as a result. Above all, relax and be yourself. Each person you see will be hoping that your folio will be filled with fresh and exciting new work with just the right commercial edge. The goodwill is there, so don't let nervousness make you behave unnaturally – don't babble or be aggressively cocky and overconfident, or mute and sulky with apprehension that your work won't be liked. *It* may be, but *you* won't be. It's as embarrassing for the client as it is for you if what you present is of poor quality or inappropriate for their needs, but they will always offer constructive criticism if they feel you genuinely welcome it.

Dress in your usual and most comfortable way but never be scruffy or purposely untidy – if you turn up covered in ink blots, perhaps that's how your work will appear, and art buyers may not want to take that chance. Most important, don't be too overcome by the need to "look like an artist." If, underneath all the junk shop clothes, flowing hair, green lipstick and carefully paint-splattered jeans, there was a genuinely imaginative illustrator who could *draw*, there would never be any shortage of talented people to carry out commissions. In

SOME IMPORTANT DON'TS

It takes a great deal of courage to admit that the work you are offered is beyond your capabilities – it takes the adoption of a truly professional attitude to point out that, while your own speciality is the sensitive portrayal of children in realistic settings and situations, the little boy in the story becomes a BMX champion and you simply can't do all those bicycles! Again, honesty will pay off in later relations with the client. Remember:

Don't ever take a job that you haven't got time to do well, either because of previous commitments or because the client's deadline is unrealistic. (Your other work will suffer as well.)

Don't take a job that you know is outside your capabilities (the client may have asked the wrong person!).

Don't take a job of which you disapprove; if you're fed up with stories in which little girls cry and little boys climb trees – or vice versa! – don't take on yet another one. If stereotyping in any form seems to turn too many books into empty political tracts rather than literature reflecting the rounded lives of real and complex people, protest. Don't lend your skills to propaganda – children's books should be free of it.

Don't take on an impossible or badly paid job and complain about it later – complain at the beginning.

Don't deliver a job with which you are dissatisfied hoping it will do – it may well do for the client, but it won't do for yourself.

SELF-PROMOTION

Self-promotion aids can come in many forms. The simplest are black and white or color xeroxes of individual pieces – but it is now possible to print cards or small posters printed at reasonable cost. Cards, from postcard size up to 8½ x 11in, can be printed black one side and color the other. (Your work needs to be in transparency form for the printer and your text details neatly typed.) A single 8½ x 11in or 8½ x 14in sheet will carry even more full-color samples on good quality paper – but bigger poster sizes may be too large to store or pin up and much too expensive for a young artist. The idea is to *keep* your work under the art director's eye, and, from the images pinned to my own wall board, the printed card would seem to be the most successful reminder of the artists I've recently seen. Get them printed *before* you begin your round of visits.

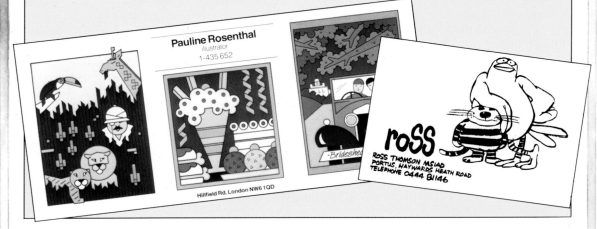

fact, the opposite is more likely to be true – it's usually the people who look like bank clerks who present folios filled with skill, imagination, surprise and true eccentricity.

If, however, you've been careful about your presentation and your work is liked, then you'll find that you need to have something representative to leave behind with clients and agents. Art buyers will ask for a sample for their files – those famous art files which are kept by publishers, advertising agencies and agents. It may seem as though your work will just disappear into a great "black hole" never to emerge again, but in fact they are generally kept up-to-date and reviewed by art buyers at regular intervals. I often go back to my files (having "built" them for several publishers) and, after a rummage around, emerge triumphant with the sample of an artist's work which had stuck in my mind and was now just what was needed – a year or so later.

Have ready some stats, a printed sheet or card with a few examples of your work in both color and black and white and your name, address and daytime telephone number. The best "calling cards" are those that are big enough to show a selection of work, yet small enough to be pinned up on the wall for easy reference.

GETTING THE WORK...

All the hard work of presentation has paid off and you have been offered your first commission. The real work is about to begin, especially for someone used to the time scale of student work who hasn't yet the experience of properly pacing their work against a professional deadline. If you've been taken on by an agent, then you'll be briefed thoroughly by the agent and may often be asked to do some sample illustrations to check the time spent on each. One successful agent, previously let down by students unable to make that leap into professional practice, sets her own jobs and deadlines to which new illustrators on her books must work. An acceptable piece must be produced by a given date before that artist's work is presented fully to clients. This is an excellent practice that publishers themselves simply haven't the time to pursue – and, of course, inexperienced artists *do* sometimes fail to produce the same quality work under the pressure of a deadline that they were able to produce in the more relaxed conditions of their student years. Books, however, provide the best apprenticeship of all, as deadlines are longish and art directors do *try* to build in enough time for a few false starts or delays.

The best clients will augment these basics with other material: a page flat-plan, galley paste-up to show the *exact* sizes and shapes of the required illustrations, or, if *you* are to lay out the pages to arrange the best layout for your drawings, then the designer's full text specification and a specimen page. The brief for a nonfiction title should be accompanied by author's notes and as much reference material as possible. If the artist is required to do *all* the research, that must be reflected in the fee, as, of course, should any hand separations of finished artwork for the printer.

If you are *not* given a written brief, take your own notes and, if any of the points listed above is not adequately covered, ask questions. Some clients explain things well, others badly – some are unable to explain themselves at all and tend to rely on an "I'll-know-it's-right-when-I-see-it" philosophy. Art directors and editors sometimes need to be reminded that artists are not clairvoyant. Don't leave until you understand exactly what you are required to do. If you feel uneasy about the deadline, say so. It's essential not to get over-enthusiastic because you've been offered a job and make unrealistic promises. You *must* give yourself the time to make some mistakes and these are inevitable during your first few jobs. The publisher will respect your concern more than an over-confident air which is not borne out by events. It is a good

---

CHECKLIST FOR A BRIEF

When you are working directly for the client you should be given a clear written brief, covering all the following points:

1. **The nature of the job:** illustrations and cover, illustrations only, cover only, etc, for a book of fiction/nonfiction. All relevant text to be provided.

2. **Specification:** size, extent, paper, printing, etc of book.

3. **Quantity:** specific number of pieces of work to be done – including cover.

4. **Media:** line or full-color, line and flat color or mixed media, and any special requirements for printing – halftones, tints, etc.

5. **Presentation:** sizes, proportions, on paper for scanning, board, film or other special requirements.

6. **Deadlines:** due date for pencil or color roughs, due date for finished artwork in agreed manner.

7. **Fee:** flat fee or advance on royalty. You should receive a contract or letter of agreement *before* beginning work on a job.

deal more professional to present a finished, well-executed job to deadline after a reasonable work-time than to promise miracles of speed and fail miserably. So speak up now!

Money

Publishers are well-known for their reluctance to talk about money – a vulgar topic in a gentlemanly world. The more highbrow and literary the house, the worse this problem is. Although the situation has improved *very* greatly over the past 20 years, you can still find yourself on the sidewalk outside happily clutching a manuscript and a sheaf of notes and still not know when, if, or how much you are likely to be paid. Don't let this happen. The proposed fee will be noted in your written brief from a good publisher. If it isn't, or you haven't been given a written brief, ask before you agree to take the job. If it's too little, haggle. While it is certainly true that the print runs for children's books are lower than for adult books and the budgets are smaller, it is also true that illustration plays a much greater role in the success of a children's book. So don't work for prestige only!

In well-run houses, the book has been costed before it reaches the point where artwork is commissioned, and so the budget for artwork is known. If the budget figure is too low to cover the amount of work involved, try to reduce the number of drawings and the complexity of the layout. For example, a big double-spread may be better than two separate full-page illustrations covering the same chapter. Be friendly but firm during all negotiations and don't fall for the line that, "If you don't want it, then someone else will." Shake hands and leave so that the publisher can get on and talk to that "someone else" who can work for unrealistic fees.

However, once you *have* agreed on an acceptable fee then forget it, and do the job for your own personal satisfaction. Don't skimp – it's your reputation that matters.

PROFESSIONAL PROTECTION

Join the appropriate professional association. The Graphic Artists Guild has made enormous strides in protecting the rights of illustrators – and educating illustrators in those rights. And the Society of Illustrators provides a wide range of social and educational programs for artists working in all fields. The Author's League of America and Poets & Writers offer assistance to all writers. The Children's Book Council is an organization set up to deal specifically with authors and illustrators of children's books. The Society of Children's Book Writers provides details of what publishers are looking for.

For legal advice try Volunteer Lawyers for the Arts in New York City; they can direct you to similar services in a number of other cities including Chicago, San Francisco, and Houston. All provide free legal services to individuals and organizations satisfying the income requirements. The Joint Ethics Committee mediates or arbitrates disputes between graphic artists and clients.

Addresses for the organizations listed above appear in the *Appendix,* page 138. *Literary Marketplace* also lists organizations for writers.

Chapter 6

Making the Book – Technique and Production

Now you can begin the most pleasant of all tasks – reading the manuscript of a children's book for the purpose of creating a series of illustrations to complement and illuminate the author's original idea. It may also be the most important part of your job, because it is during this crucial first reading that basic impressions of character, atmosphere, setting and plot will form.

READ AND PLAN

1. Read the text simply for the story first – and for enjoyment. On your second reading begin to *make notes*: physical details of the characters, setting, period details if any, and an outline of the sequence of events broken down to relate the number of illustrations required. For storybooks, novels and picture books the early illustrations will be scene-setters.

2. Against your outline begin to *make little thumbnail sketches*, showing which elements of the story will be included in each. You'll be surprised how often the composition you have created at this stage in a few swift pencil lines is the one that becomes the structure of a finished illustration.

3. For longer books, where most of the pages have text and you are fitting your illustrations into more formal pages with blocks of text balanced by lively areas of illustration, it's best to *make a flat-plan*, if one hasn't been provided. Draw up the required number of spreads on a large layout sheet – or use a printed pad of "dummy plans" –

then design in sketch form the way the illustrations will fall on the page. Variety is important, and you will want to make your strongest visual statements coincide with the climaxes or high points of action in the author's story.

4. If you've been given a set of galleys and some full-sized dummy sheets, you can do the same with the full-sized elements. *Tack the cut-out areas of text down lightly* until you are pleased with the final position and rhythm of the pages.

5. If you are working on a picture book, *make a small paper dummy* in the same size (or to the same proportions) as the final book. You can often work in a printer's blank dummy prepared for the publisher's production department. This gives you the feel of the *real* book – its size, shape, binding style and paper. Sketch in the details of each of your planned pages and paste in the text galley or draw in the line (or few lines) of text.

YOUR PRIVATE REFERENCE LIBRARY

Once you are happy with the layout, then go back to your notes – and list any references you need. It will take the rest of your career to build a really comprehensive reference library of your own, but the sooner you start, the less time you'll spend rushing to the library for last-minute loans. The foundations of a good working reference library should be laid in your student years – items cut from magazines and newspapers, and photographs taken with a polaroid while out on "observational-drawing" assignments. Add to those good habits the one of looking in secondhand bookshops for bargains and haunt local junkshops. While you're adding some terrific "period piece" to your wardrobe, add a few books or magazines as well – back numbers of *National Geographic*, *Life* or *People* and the individual volumes of incomplete part-works can be had quite cheaply and provide a wealth of wonderful source material.

Don't just look for the references you need for *this* job but pick up anything that interests you in the hope that it will be of use in future jobs. Storage will swiftly become a problem but you *can* cut up everything and put it into filing cabinets or folders. Only attempt this, however, if you have a real *passion* for organization. Alternatively, once you've filled all the walls with bookshelves, build two even piles of the biggest and heaviest books and rest your drawing board on them – inspiration will then never be far away.

When you come to the end of your career

SAMPLE LAYOUTS

For books with lots of text, make a flat-plan, sketching in where the illustrations are to fall on each page.

Vary the arrangement of text and pictures to create impact.

The artist in his studio surrounded by a lifetime of references, as imagined by Fritz Wegner.

and publishers are all too young to remember your work, you'll be able to take the advice of Fritz Wegner, brilliant illustrator and quite uncanny discoverer of printed treasures of every kind, and set yourself up as a second-hand book dealer to see you through your old age. The best of your student finds may be well worth a small fortune by that time.

BEWARE INFRINGEMENT

A word of warning: photographs in books and magazines are an excellent reference tool but *don't* base your illustrations directly on any printed photographs because:

1. You'll be infringing on the photographers' copyright.

2. They are easily recognized by art directors and editors who become very familiar with visual references.

3. Copying (or tracing) directly from a photograph produces a wooden, lifeless illustration, and kills inspiration. Take your *own* photographs and use them for reference only – several photos of different details of a drawing or a series of poses by a model can help to build the illustration in the round even if its eventual life is in a two-dimensional reproduction on a flat page. Great artists from da Vinci to Norman Rockwell have used visual aids to create paintings of depth and reality.

PREPARING THE ROUGHS

Having sketched out the basic composition for each page or spread, and collected *all* the necessary reference material, you can now make detailed pencil roughs for each illustration. This is when all the important decisions are made: the physical characteristics of the characters, their clothes, setting and the portrayal of action and incident. Read the text again *and again* – until there is no detail that can have slipped through unnoticed. Everything should now be in your notes. Children, as well as authors, *do* notice when the little girl in the story is said to have short black curly hair and the illustration shows a long blond ponytail. Take the trouble to get it right! You will be fitting your style of drawings and choice of palette to that of the writer – realistic or humorous, loose, relaxed and painterly, soft and moody, or sharp, angular and brightly colored. Of course, you will have been chosen for the commission because of your own particular style, but each book you illustrate will need to be considered for *its* own special content and atmosphere. As you become more skillful, you'll be able to add more variation and subtlety to your original "personal" style. Using the same style year in and year out will be deadening for you as an illustrator, and your own enjoyment *is* a necessary part of a job well done.

The more detailed and "finished" your pencil roughs, the easier it is to complete the illustrations to the satisfaction of the client. Not everyone can "read" roughs – and certainly not everyone who commissions artwork. Be thorough, even pedantic, at this stage. Double-check the sizes and proportions. When showing what you intend to do, keep all your layouts and detailed notes on color and reference handy.

You may have a chance to discuss the book at this stage with the author as well as with the editor or art director. This is usually an enjoyable experience, but it can be disconcerting if you discover that the author has quite a different – and not always appropriate – visual picture of the characters and setting. I once did a book with an author whose story was a charming futuristic fantasy. When she saw the brilliant angular black and white drawing by John Vernon Lord, her reaction was surprise. *"Oh,"* she said, *"I thought the drawings would be like Ernest Shepard's!"*

If copies of the roughs are to be *sent* to the author they must be self-explanatory. Most authors are a joy to work with and truly understand – and appreciate – the artist's different, but complementary contribution to the success of the book. Any alterations should be noted, discussed and attended to at this stage.

Getting paid for roughs

If you have made a stage-payment agreement, then, when the roughs have been formally approved, you or your agent will be entitled to invoice for the work done up to rough stage. If, for some reason unconnected with the quality of your work, the book does not proceed to publication, your payment to rough stage should cover the time spent to that point. If, however, even after alterations and perhaps new roughs, your work is found unacceptable or not up to the standard requested, then a "rejection" fee will be agreed – usually a quarter of the total fee, but this varies. This situation is to be avoided – if your specimens were good enough to lead to a commission, then the chance to do some really good work shouldn't be missed. From those first few jobs you can begin to build a rapport with your satisfied clients, so that ultimately you can work with a swift shorthand of roughs and perhaps no roughs at all, for, as illustrator, you will be fully trusted to come up with an imaginative, surprising and technically proficient solution.

Working methods: Alan Lee

Each artist has a favorite way of working, often developed over many years of trial and error. Most follow the same basic method of building an illustration from a quick thumbnail sketch, which establishes the composition, through a series of ever more detailed roughs to the final illustration ready for reproduction. This process is beautifully demonstrated by Alan Lee with his step-by-step build-up of a superbly detailed painting for *The Mirrorstone*, written by Michael Palin.

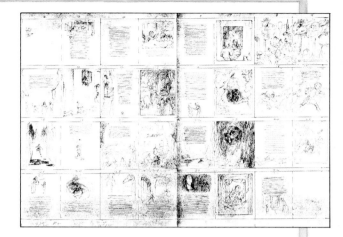

*Having read and annotated the text with research notes on costume, characters and details of place and period, the artist prepares a flat-plan for the book (**above right**). Here Alan Lee has sketched in each of the proposed illustrations balanced by blocks of text — boldly used as parts of a dynamic design whole. The spreads are planned for pace and variety with each dramatic climax carefully placed. Decisions are made at this stage about the content and composition of each illustration but all the details are left until the thumbnail sketches are developed into full-sized roughs.*

The rough of one illustration is developed swiftly (**top left**) from the early blocking-in stages to a more settled composition. Groups of people are placed for dramatic effect and the architecture begins to take on solid forms. The shape of the drawing is now known. The small hero can just be seen in the shadowy outline at the far left of the drawing. In the final rough (**above right**) Alan Lee has substantially altered the viewer's perspective of the scene while retaining its basic character. The row of buildings creating the background have been pushed further back to give a greater depth to the "stage" upon which the scene is set. This allows him the freedom to develop the foreground and now the simple foursquare arches on the right of the earlier rough have become the porch of an inn — complete with musicians and an appreciative audience. The small hero is still in his place, almost lost among all this bustle, and this is where he remains. Alan Lee uses a carefully controlled palette to bring the final painting to life.

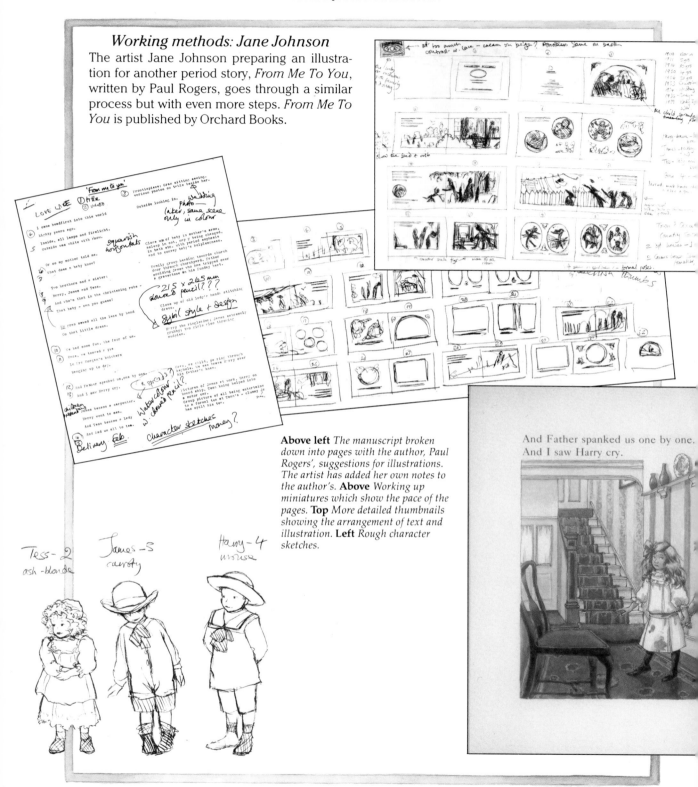

Working methods: Jane Johnson

The artist Jane Johnson preparing an illustration for another period story, *From Me To You*, written by Paul Rogers, goes through a similar process but with even more steps. *From Me To You* is published by Orchard Books.

Above left The manuscript broken down into pages with the author, Paul Rogers', suggestions for illustrations. The artist has added her own notes to the author's. **Above** Working up miniatures which show the pace of the pages. **Top** More detailed thumbnails showing the arrangement of text and illustration. **Left** Rough character sketches.

And Father spanked us one by one.
And I saw Harry cry.

Left *Sketching in characters and backdrop in a first rough.* **Below** *The rough refined, and detail added: the painting begins to take shape.*

And Father spanked us one by one.
And I saw Harry cry.

Below *The finished painting. The preparation work has been carefully and professionally executed and this is reflected in the final illustration.*

LAYOUT: THE TERROR OF THE WHITE PAPER

The book you are illustrating may be a picture book, a storybook, an older children's novel or a nonfiction book in which your illustrations may find themselves sharing the page with text, captions, diagrams and even photographs. The range of content, format and extent is so great that virtually every new book or series has its own special layout requirements. There are, however, a few important rules to follow no matter *what* kind of book you're doing.

A "formal" picture-book layout. The lines of text on the verso are centered in a large white space with a full-page illustration opposite.

The landscape format lends itself to a very imaginative use of both text lines and illustrative details. The sky is put to excellent use as a "billboard" for the signwriter's art.

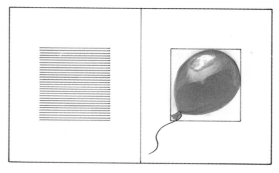

A more balanced formality — the longer text makes a block of gray (black lines on white) which is matched by a panel, squared-up illustration of the same size and shape.

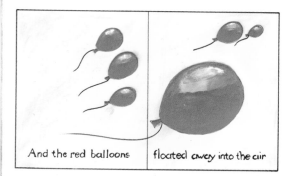

A few words of text, broken into key phrases, set in a large, often sans serif typeface. They are placed either at the top or the bottom of a large, open spread dominated by the illustration.

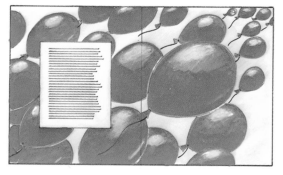

The text of a liberally illustrated storybook or book of poems or folk takes is treated as a panel — a cool rectangular shape making a window in a full-bled double-page illustration.

SIMPLE RULES FOR GOOD LAYOUT...

1. *The text must be clear and readable on every page or spread.* This is *especially* important in books for the very young for whom the recognition of a few words in large, clear type helps to begin the process of reading. Don't let your illustrations "grow" to fill the page areas so that there is too little room for the text. Too many good books have poor typography printed illegibly over areas of strong or broken color. Even author/artists do this, fighting an internal battle for the available space.

2. *The content of text and illustration must be compatible.* What the text *says* is happening on a given page must be what happens – or is suggested – in the illustration. Don't get the pictures out of sync with the story and don't give away what happens on the following page. Make *each* spread a new and surprising combination of complementary elements complete within itself.

3. *The design of the page is there to serve the reader and isn't an end in itself.* Good design is inconspicuous and seems to flow naturally from the story and style of illustration. The design may be the responsibility of the illustrator or of an in-house designer and ideally they should work together to find the best design solution for each book or series.

4. *Text and illustrations should be used with variety and imagination to enhance the action or atmosphere of the story.* Books may be either "portrait" (taller than wide) or "landscape" (wider than tall) in format, but a spread of portrait pages can be used for a long landscape illustration, while a two-column text arrangement on a landscape page allows for several "portrait" illustrations.

5. *The pace and drama of a story can be enhanced by an appropriate and exciting page layout.* Some examples are shown on this spread.

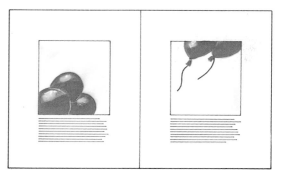

Two small miniature illustrations with their text placed intimately below.

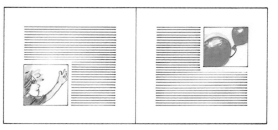

In a longer text, where illustrations occur at regular intervals, the pictures may be "spots" dropped in at an appropriate place in the story with text running round them.

THE RIGHT STYLE FOR THE RIGHT JOB

In your first discussions with the client you will probably have settled on the final form in which the illustrations will appear. In the broadest terms, you will know whether they need to be in crisp black and white line with open hatching for use in small-format paperback printing on poor quality paper, black and white fine line and tone for a hardback novel on good quality paper, or full color for a picture or information book. Any special requirements should be noted: the artwork *must* be same size because of series printing; it *must* be hand-separated because of cost; or it *must* have black line on a separate overlay to combine with text in several languages. All these details should appear on your written brief or in your own notes. But, when you get to the finished artwork stage, there will still be final decisions to be made about *how* your detailed roughs can best be translated into the kind of illustrations which best convey the mood and atmosphere of the author's story.

There are a bewildering number of ways in which to tackle even the simplest line job (anything from a one-column spot for a magazine to a series of small chapter heads for a cookbook). You can use a classic pen and ink technique to produce a loose sketch drawing which depends upon freshness and immediacy (by the way, don't be fooled, only a master draftsman can produce a drawing like this at the first try). A thicker "slow-line" drawing, defining the outside of strong clear shapes with a rough, scrambled line is wonderful for tactile things like food, kitchen utensils or toys. A vigorous line drawn with waterproof ink and then painted over and "shadowed" with light washes of thinned ink or watercolor gives both shape and atmosphere to a narrative drawing, such as boats bobbing on an oily sea under darkening clouds, figures walking in a wood, a cat asleep on a hearth or warm sunlit stones.

If your technique is good enough for wood engraving, wood- or lino-cut, silkscreen print or lithography, then the "print" quality of these craft techniques will add another dimension to illustrations for books, magazines and especially posters and other large display items. For color work the only limit to the range of technical possibilities is your own skill and imagination.

New products are constantly being introduced which are both seductive and expensive. During any good art school course you will no doubt have spent some time learning to handle the basic techniques of pencil, watercolor, gouache, oil crayon, pastels and the various forms of acrylic paint. If you *still* can't lay down a watercolor wash then practice until you can.

If you can draw, you can draw with *anything*: sticks, pens, conté, chalk, wax crayons, brushes or your finger in the sand! If you *can't* draw, then you won't succeed as an illustrator.

And because he loved it, he broke off the bloom.

The breathtaking mastery of both technique and color combine to maximum effect in Joseph's Yard, *one of Charles Keeping's most powerful picture books* (**far left**). *In* The Bear's Water Picnic *by John Yeoman and Quentin Blake, the illustrator uses his line to superb effect; strong, descriptive and deceptively simple. Blake's technique is the result of years of refinement. Tony Ross is another master craftsman who uses the basic line and wash technique.* Stone Soup (**below**) *is typical of his work — the line itself manages to convey his sharp humor, while the color gives a glowing warmth which takes away the sting.*

Drawing is fundamental to everything else in illustration, and is the *one* skill an illustrator cannot do without. Draw constantly.

Draw everywhere and anywhere. A small sketchbook, with a pen or pencil in your pocket (cartridge pens are a blessing here) at all times, helps you to record interesting visual data – good faces, hands, details of architecture, landscape and the minutiae of daily life for later use in illustrations. Sometimes, it is the absolutely accurate detail – culled from a row of filed and dated sketchbooks – that makes the final illustration and gives it genuine atmosphere and authenticity.

Different approaches

It is essential to choose a technique and general style for the finished drawings which is appropriate to the plot and atmosphere of the story. As Catherine Storr points out in Chapter 1, it is misleading to choose the wrong narrative style when writing the story. It is equally wrong to use an unsympathetic illustration technique. If your version of *Cinderella* is a light-hearted romantic comedy, it needs a light-hearted warm colored style; if you want to emphasize only the tragic aspects of cruelty, loneliness and the deprivation suffered by the luckless Cinderella, then your choice of color tones and the medium in which they are used will be very different. Here are some styles you might use:

Left *Cinderella rendered as a silhouette figure, a drawing style made popular in the 18th century. The artist is limited in the amount he or she can convey using this approach. For instance, facial expressions are impossible; any message needs to be carried in the outline of the figure. Silhouette works best on a small scale, rather than when there is a large area to fill.*

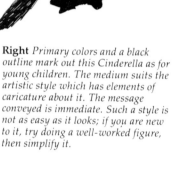

Right *Primary colors and a black outline mark out this Cinderella as for young children. The medium suits the artistic style which has elements of caricature about it. The message conveyed is immediate. Such a style is not as easy as it looks; if you are new to it, try doing a well-worked figure, then simplify it.*

Right *The artist has used colored pencils to create this romantic, realistic Cinderella. Colored pencils allow areas of light and shade to be created using the technique of hatching. This gives depth to the creation, and is a pleasing effect.*

Left *A highly stylized Cinderella. Here pen and ink have been used to create a clean, crisp image but one without depth. Although it has not been explored here to its full extent, this is medium which allows the artist to put in as much detail as he or she wants.*

Left *Here the artist has used the moody medium of watercolor. The translucent quality of watercolor allows the application of several layers, thereby creating tone. Again, this is a medium that can be as loose or as tight as you want.*

Below *The time-consuming technique of stippling has been used to create tone on this figure.*

Above *Using brush and ink, the artist has given this form a rough, sketchy quality. The rendering appears haphazard and off-the-cuff, in part due to the chosen medium — though ink and wash can give a more controlled line. This is a loose, immediate style that would be most appropriate to a retelling that broke the traditional mold.*

Media and technique

Felt pens and markers now come in all shapes, sizes and colors with soft, pointed or square-cut tips. They are great for the really rapid sketch when time doesn't allow more, and they have their now-traditional use as "visualizing" tools in the planning stages of an advertising or poster campaign. But for book illustration they have their hazards, also. They are too "easy" and make too slick a line, covering the paper so rapidly that there isn't time to think the drawing out carefully. Children use them instinctively and well, but adult illustrators need more "friction" and a medium that occasionally fights back.

Colored pencils, pastels and crayons have become increasingly popular with illustrators, especially since the separation techniques of modern scanning cameras have become more and more sophisticated. Now the printed results from the layers of soft pencil lines (laid over one another in a simple direction or cross-hatched in patterns) are even more subtle. Almost anything can now be faithfully reproduced and even those troublesome greens and oranges reproduce with astonishing accuracy. Fluorescent and metallic inks are still not really reproducible – but then, they rarely add anything to the quality of an original illustration either. Gold, silver and colored metallic blockings are easy to use, and the technique of blocking titles in a metallic color has been used effectively on paperback covers for many years.

When choosing the medium to use for your finished illustrations, consider the style you have established in your roughs (and which properly interprets the style and "tone" of the text). If a lighthearted cartoon style is to be used, you'll want to execute it with a light touch and with strong clear color – not a style well suited to a heavyweight medium such as oil paint, but excellent in ink line and light watercolor washes (best exemplified by the work of Quentin Blake). A book with a strong "design" element and large areas of flat color might well lend itself to a combination of drawn silhouettes and cut paper or fabric collage (both used superbly by artists such as Leo Leonni and Jan Pienkowski). There will be a right style for each job.

LIFE HISTORY OF A BOOK

Basically the life history of a book runs like this:

1. The text is accepted and the author is contracted.

2. Decisions are made in house about the best type of format, extent and illustrations – a request for costings (including as much information as possible) is sent to the production department. Unit cost is crucial in the future planning and production of the book. Artists are considered and samples are looked at.

3. The costings are received. The book is edited and designed (if the artist is to be provided with galleys to work from).

4. The artist is commissioned and contracted. (If the book is a picture book the artist may well discuss layout and illustration with the author, editor and art director at this stage, and may work from the manuscript, deciding on typographic as well as illustration style.) The artist gets a full brief and all support material.

5. The artist submits roughs which are discussed and approved with or without further additions and alterations. Text galleys are corrected and film, or paper repro, ordered.

6. The artist delivers the finished artwork, occasionally in full camera ready copy (CRC) form – but usually as finished illustrations with a rough layout.

7. The designer prepares a full CRC dummy or make-up dummy to show position of all text and illustrations. The text will appear as film or repro. All instructions for the printer are included on the dummy.

THE MYSTERY OF MANUFACTURE

What happens to your illustrations after you've delivered them, had them approved and accepted and pocketed the fee or advance due on delivery? Months go by (seems like years and occasionally *is*!) before you see the finished product in book form. If you're lucky, you'll be kept in touch with the various stages of production and have the opportunity to check color proofs and see revises. As your reputation grows you'll be in a position to *insist* upon as much further involvement as you wish, but in the beginning you may find that you aren't consulted as much as you'd like.

In an ideal situation you will be working with an experienced and knowledgeable art director or children's editor, but this is by no means a certainty. Before children's books became "big business," the editorial staff handling the children's list did *all* the jobs concerned, armed often with nothing but a bachelor's degree in English and a typing course. Then, over the years, many of them gained an encyclopedic knowledge of print technology. During the earlier postwar years, the non-specialist editor was often, luckily,

working with an extremely well-trained artist familiar with all the techniques needed by the commercial illustrator.

However, as more specialist staff have moved into the children's book publishing field, the art training of future illustrators has moved away from technique and technology, concerning itself more with theory than practice – with the result that students often know *less* about the profession they hope to enter than ever before. And publishers, too, have not *all* seen the necessity to have specialist staff or even specialist training for staff working with illustration, a highly complex subject. You *may* find that you know more than the person who commissions you.

American artists have long been the best-informed technically because they have been hand-separating full-color artwork for decades – and are still doing it! For 20-odd years artists in Europe have had virtually everything done for them – a technological holiday! Don't let print technology remain a mystery to you.

8. Color proofs – in imposed pages or as scatter proofs – arrive from printer to be checked against originals by artist and art director or editor. All placings of illustration and text are checked on imposed proofs. Color proofs returned.

9. Revised color proofs if needed. Final film sent from the repro house to the printer, then "blue" ozalid proofs are checked for order placement. The book is passed for press.

10. The books are printed. Running sheets sent for final color check.

11. The books are bound.

12. The books leave the factory on their way to the publisher's warehouse.

A make-up dummy spread to show position of text and illustrations.

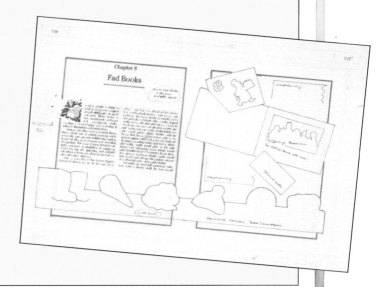

GUTTERS, FLUSHES, IMPOSITIONS AND THE RUN-AROUND
A BEGINNER'S GUIDE TO PRINT TERMINOLOGY

Align: to line up lines of text, or lines of text with illustrations or photographs in a layout.

Back-up: to print on the back of a printed sheet (4 backed 1 means printed 4 colors on one side of the sheet and 1 color – usually black – on the other).

Bleed: the area of printed image that extends beyond the "reproduction area" of a piece of artwork or printed image before it is trimmed to page size.

Blow-up: an enlargement from a small original.

Blues: the proof provided by the printer (after all **color corrections** have been made and film prepared) to show that all elements have been placed in the correct order and sequence.

Body type: the type normally used for the body or main text of a book – not captions or headings. The size range is usually from 6 to 16 point. (Picture books may have a body-type size up to 30 pt.)

Bulk: the thickness of paper – spine widths are calculated from paper bulk and number of pages.

Case: the boards and spine of a hardbound or "cased" book.

Character count: the number of single letters, punctuation marks and spaces in a piece of **copy.**

Characters: individual letters, figures, punctuation marks and spaces, etc.

Color correction a) by an art director or editor: checking **color proofs** against original copy to check faithfulness and quality of color; and b) by the printer after checking: adjusting the color balance by dot-correction handwork, masking-out or scanning.

Color proofs: proofs pulled from proofing plates at an early stage of the production process to check quality and faithfulness of color – they may be imposed with text and pages in correct order or as random "scatter" proofs.

Color separation: isolating each color hue and value in a multicolor work onto separate films by hand or photographic process. Most full-color artwork printed by *offset litho* is separated into four basic colors: yellow, magenta (red), cyan (blue) and black. Occasionally a fifth color is added for flat backgrounds.

Continuous tone: an illustration (photograph, wash drawing, or painting) consisting of a broad range of tone or gradation of tones.

Copy: manuscript, color or line artwork or photographs to be reproduced; often copy is used as a synonym for text *only* and the term "art" applied to all artwork.

Cover: the thin board binding of a paperback book.

Crop: any portion of photograph or artwork to be left out in the reproduction, or to eliminate portions of a photograph or artwork by the use of cropmarks.

CRC: camera ready copy – paste-up with text repro and artwork ready for the camera.

Die-cut: steel cutting rules bent to image shapes which are cut into board or paper – used in novelty books and pop-ups and for "shaped" board books.

Display type: any type other than body copy designed to catch attention, for example, heads and titles, often unusual, highly decorated or photographically distorted faces in sizes from 16 to 72 pt.

Dry-mounting: using tissue or wax under heat and pressure to mount drawings or photographs on board.

Dummy: a) the blank book prepared by the printer to give an example of the format, binding style and paper weight of a proposed job (perfect for sketchbooks); and b) the rough layout to show positioning of illustrations and text.

Em: in typography, the square of a type body size.

En: half an em.

Flop: to print left to right to show image facing in opposite direction – either to change emphasis in the artwork or because printer has reversed artwork original or photograph (check content – some pictures just *don't* reverse because of type, logos, familiar landmarks or objects, such as watches, etc.).

Fluorescent inks: inks in special colors with fluorescent qualities – very bright (one of those good ideas you'll wish you hadn't had – expensive and troublesome to use for little gain).

Flush left or right: type set to line up at left or right of a column.

Folio: page number.

Format: the shape and size of a book (and sometimes the binding style and overall layout of the page).

Galley proof: originally a proof taken from a "galley" – the compositor's form – now usually a copy of a continuous column of photo- or computer-set type, for text correction and paste-up purposes.

Gutter: the margin on the inner edge of a page between the text or picture area and the binding, or the area across the central binding of the book – i.e. in library bindings the gutter is "pinched in" by up to $7/16$ in.

Grain: the direction in which the fibers lie in a piece of paper – some strongly-textured papers can add interesting effects to washes, and shadows to watercolor paintings.

Halftone: printing tone illustrations by breaking them down photographically into dots used in both **letterpress** printing and **lithography.**

Head margin: the white space above the first line at the top of the page.

Hickeys: the specks on color proofs caused by dirt or imperfections on printing plates.

Hue: basic body color without shades or tints.

Image: (in a book context) the area of artwork or photography which is to be reproduced and neither trimmed nor cropped from page or cover when reproduced.

Imposition: the plan for placing pages on a printing sheet so that when folded, each page will be in the proper sequence. Books are prepared in signatures of 16, 24 or 32 pages – always multiples of 4 – folded from a single sheet (24-page picture books can be printed as a single 24-page signature).

Jacket: the outer detachable cover or "dustjacket" on a hardback book. Some hardback picture books have *both* printed paper **covers** pasted onto the boards *and* a separate jacket.

Justify: to space out type lines so that they are even on the left and right.

Keyline: inked lines on artwork which indicate edges, borders or areas where the printer is to add color as a mechanical screen. Some keylines print in black or color, others reverse to white and others mark edges of colored image area but do not print – as indicated on the overlay or marginal instructions.

Laminate: the plastic film heat-bonded to a **cover** or **jacket** which heightens color, gives a glossy surface and protects the cover board from damage. Also used on wipe-off pages in children's puzzle and activity books.

Layout: the drawings, rough plan or sketches of the pages of a book to show the relative positions of text and illustrations.

Letterpress: method of relief printing in which the printing surface is higher than the non-printing surface, used for printing text or coarse halftone black and white line drawings.

Line copy: any artwork which can be reproduced without using a screen process.

Lithography: the method of printing now most commonly used for illustrated books. The printing surface is on the same level as the non-printing surface with oil separating the different areas. Used for full-color or fine-toned original artwork and books with integrated text and pictures. In **offset litho** a rubber blanket is used to offset ink from plates to paper.

Manuscript (ms): originally a handwritten script but now used to mean all the copy for a particular book ready for editing, design and setting, whether typed or printed from a word processor.

Mark-up: preparing a manuscript for printing, refers to copy editing and typographic mark-up. The instructions for size, typeface and "house-style" of setting in the margin.

Mechanical: the finished paste-up of all the elements of a book or cover in position and form ready for photo mechanical reproduction (**CRC**).

Overlay: a) a sheet of layout or visualizing paper placed over artwork for protection and to carry instructions and notes for the printer; b) when artwork is separated by the artist, the various color and line areas are prepared in shades of black on separate acetate or Kodatrace overlays and registered in position.

Pica: the standard unit of measurement in typography – ⅙ of an inch or 12 points.

Plates: a) blocks used to print line illustrations by **letterpress;** b) flexible sheets of metal, plastic or paper used in **offset litho** printing; c) illustrations printed on art paper gathered in a separate section or inserted page by page.

PMTs: photomechanical transfers – produced to repro sizes used in CRC.

Prelims: the pages usually at the beginning of a book consisting of half-title, title page, imprint page, contents and any other pre-text material such as acknowledgments and introduction.

Progressives: printers' proofs showing the inking of each of the colors in the four-color process so that color-weight can be checked.

Proportion: the relationship of the original size of artwork to the actual final reproduction size in both height and width – photographs are usually scaled up and artwork is usually prepared larger and scaled down (but should always be done in the correct proportion – i.e. ¼, ½ or twice up – so that the instruction to the printer is 75 per cent, 66⅓ per cent or 50 per cent of size). A small reduction in size can often enhance a drawing, giving it greater crispness. Enlarging artwork gives it a looser, more open feel but "washes out" color.

Recto: right-hand page (page one of a book is *always* a recto as are all odd-numbered pages).

Register marks (or crossmarks): marks to show the exact fitting, in position, of two or more color **overlays,** or line overlays to show final placing of elements in mechanical **CRC.** Marks also appear on the later **color proofs** and running sheets.

Rough: the pencil sketches for drawings or paintings to show content, composition and color notes for discussion with commissioning art director or editor before going on to the finished artwork.

Reverse: the switch from black or color to white.

Reverse out: instruction to printer that lines of type, **keyline** rules or specific images are to appear as white in a toned or four-color proof.

Run-around: type set to a narrower width than rest of text to fit around an illustration.

Stet: proofreader's mark meaning "let it stand"; a previous reader's marks or corrections can be reversed or cancelled with a stet.

Verso: left-hand page (page two of a book is *always* a verso as are all even-numbered pages).

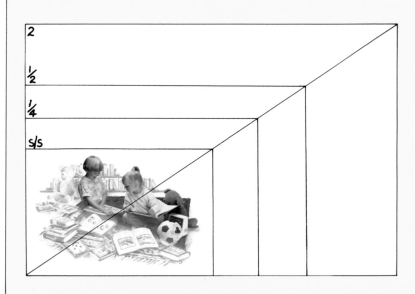

Illustrations are usually drawn larger than the actual size required. The style or accuracy of the illustration will determine how much bigger the artwork should be. The diagonal line is an easy way to scale artwork up or down as the ratio of the vertical to the horizontal remains the same.

PROTECTION: FOR YOURSELF AND YOUR ARTWORK

For every job – no matter how small or how little it earns – always prepare and present your work in the most professional way, correctly sized, mounted and protected. The reproduction of clean, well-covered work will be of better quality and the original returned to you in better condition. Make it easy for publishers and printers to handle your work with care.

Do each piece of line or color work on a separate piece of flexible board or strong paper mounted (at the corners only) on board for protection. Leave an outer margin of no more than 2in around each finished drawing and mark the artwork *NOT TO BE TRIMMED*. For convenience and economy, printers will group all artworks which are to be reproduced in the same size or to the same proportion, and these huge, elegant areas of white around your drawings will simply be trimmed away. They are wasteful and costly, not least to you. Conserve your supplies of board for the next job! Equally don't make your drawings too big or put several small drawings on one large sheet – they are too easily damaged. A set of uniformly book-sized boards carefully packed stands the best chance of survival through the whole manufacturing process.

Cover each piece with clear layout or visualizing paper. Notes to the printer from you and the publisher, noting size and any special proofing requirements, should be noted on these overlay sheets. They do, however, sometimes get removed or torn, so *on each board* write:

1. The title of the book and publisher.

2. The chapter and page reference on ms or paste-up.

3. The size or proportion for reproduction. For example, "S/S" or "100 per cent of size," "3 to 2" or "reduce to 2½in wide," "to be 12in deep" or any other designation you choose to indicate size of original to size of reproduction.

4. Your name, making it easier for the work to be returned to you when the book has been printed.

If you make it obvious that *you* respect your work, then the other people through whose hands it will pass – publishers, repro house and printers – will also respect it.

For protection, mount artwork on board. Notes to the printer go on the overlay.

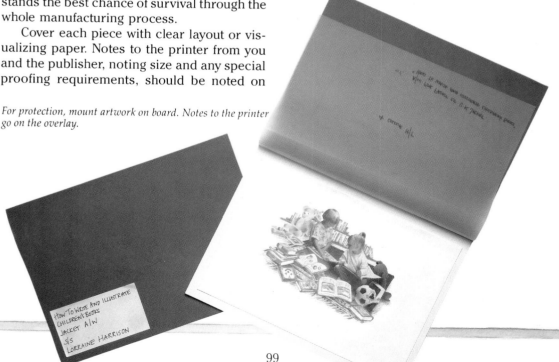

YOUR RIGHTS IN LAW

When you create a piece of artwork or write a text for a book or magazine – whether commissioned or speculative – both the copyright and the ownership of your own work remain with you. A line to that effect should appear on the copyright page: *illustrations © A. Nother, 1988*, but even if it does not, the copyright belongs to the creator. When you accept a commission to do illustrations for a book in exchange for a flat fee or an advance and a royalty on future sales, in effect, you license the publisher to reproduce your work in a certain number of editions of a named book in certain countries. Under the terms of the agreement you make with the publisher – and each book or series will have its own special set of terms – the publisher may be paying you for volume rights (*all* editions = higher fee) or just hardback rights for one country (= lower fee with extra payments for further rights sold for paperback or foreign editions as these occur). A flat fee agreement *does not* mean that you relinquish your copyright *unless* you have specifically agreed to this. If you are asked – or required – to sell your work outright to the publisher (many educational publishers do require this) and the fee quoted is large enough to cover this, then you may choose to do so – especially if you are unlikely to be able to sell the pieces individually later. Books with prestige or high "artistic" value may well have a second life as collectors' pieces. If, however, you *don't* formally sign away the rights in your work, then they remain with you.

The general "rule of thumb" for advertising work is that the client buys both the artwork and all the rights in that artwork outright, but advertising fees are generous enough to allow for this. Publishing fees rarely are, and the extra income generated by reprints and second rights sales is both welcome and necessary to an artist who prefers bookwork to any other form of illustration.

When the job has been printed, the artwork should be sent back to you. Having agreed to sell the publishing rights in the work, however, you cannot sell them again, *unless* and *until* those rights revert to you. You *can* sell the physical artwork itself to collectors, for increasingly attractive prices. Let your publishers know if your work is to appear for sale in an exhibition. The company will generally want to support you in this as it provides extra publicity and sales for your book. Keep a list of any purchases and, better still,

a set of reproducible prints or transparencies of the artwork for use in reprints or future new editions. You don't want to find that the book goes out of print, when plates or films wear out, because the originals were no longer available to reproduce from. Some collectors are interested in purchasing the artwork for whole books and may be willing to lend them back for a reprint. But it is much safer to keep reproducible material on hand for this.

The purchaser of your originals *does not* own either copyright or publishing rights (unless these are once again yours to sell), but only the physical originals to enjoy. He or she cannot sell printed postcards or greeting cards made from the work (or even personal Christmas cards without the permission of both you and your publisher). *Make this clear when you sell your work.* Complicated? Yes, and fraught with difficulty, but it is necessary that all parties involved know exactly who owns what!

Above all, don't feel apologetic about either questioning the terms of an agreement *or* asking for your work back at the appropriate time. The agreement should *say* when it will be available – either immediately after printing or within an agreed time if all or some of it is to be used for promotion purposes. Do check on the artwork with your client – the art director or editor should have received it promptly from the printer, checked that everything was returned in good condition, chased any missing pieces and recorded its return to you.

If a single piece or a whole book has been lost or damaged while in the care of the printer or publisher, then the artist must be compensated for its loss and a sum will be mutually agreed between publisher and artist. *Every* publisher, even the most fanatically caring and careful, has had precious originals lost or damaged during the manufacturing process. Your continuing good relations with the publisher then depend upon the efforts made to retrieve your work and, failing that, the swift processing of a claim for compensation.

Mutual respect and cooperation in the cause of good publishing is vital.

For years the British Association of Illustrators used this delightful drawing by Paul Davis as a gentle reminder to publishers that artwork belongs to the artist.

The last word: I hope you'll be encouraged to go out and *present* yourself in the most productive way; *get* the work and *do* the work with skill, efficiency, and enjoyment. Never take the easiest way to a solution but the one that best complements the spirit of the text, holds a few visual surprises and gives *you* the most job satisfaction. It may be one of the most important things you *will* get. Success itself will bring its own problems. How will you keep inventing new delights when you're continually asked to repeat the old winning ways? *Don't* get typecast or persuaded into the self-parody and facile cynicism of an often-repeated formula. You may have to persuade – or offend – your staunchest supporters by insisting on the chance to explore and extend the range of your work. *Do it!*

Book illustration may be one of the most pleasant occupations around and one of the most sought after, so make sure that your talent is backed by knowledge, professionalism and the desire to communicate with the ultimate consumer . . . the child.

Good luck!

With appreciation and special thanks to the Association of Illustrators whose spirited and unflagging support of illustrators over the past 15 years has won many important battles and forever "raised the consciousness" of the whole publishing profession.

Chapter 7

Factual Writing – Reflecting a Child's World

Why do you want to write nonfiction for children? Writing on a specific subject with children in mind is a difficult craft. It is not simply a shorter or paler version of a book for adults. The whole concept is different and the presentation, of necessity, more direct. There are two main perspectives from which you can write nonfiction for children: as a committed enthusiast or expert in a particular field, *or* you can write as a communicator, someone who can stimulate a child reader to make the most of his or her own skills and interests.

If you're an author who falls into the first of these two categories, you need to reflect upon your own early interest in the subject and ask yourself some questions:

- What first excited your interest?

- What stimulated further investigation?

- Was it adult led or dominated?

- Were other children equally fascinated?

The answers may give clues about the likely level of appeal of your own subject to a new generation of children. Writing to satisfy children – whether they are your own, young relatives or a school class – is never a completely reliable guide to subject appeal. In these circumstances, children can be fiercely loyal rather than truly honest! Like teachers, writers can sometimes be so excited by a theme that their own enthusiasm can get in the way of the presentation of the material, and a potentially stimulating lesson or book falls flat – or loses its way.

CHOOSING A SUBJECT

If you feel you write from a communicator's standpoint, then you begin with a different set of questions and assumptions. You may have selected a particular topic because contact with children has led you to believe that there is a need for a book on the subject. You then have to ask:

- What is the extent of the need?
- What or whose perspective is the correct one in the circumstances?

- Where can I find reliable and varied source material?

- Who can check its accuracy?

When writing from either position – enthusiast or communicator – it is essential to question seriously whether the proposed text will be of general interest to children.

Any interest a publisher may have in your proposal will require a positive response to that question, so spend a few hours in the public library or a bookstore to check books already written on the same or similar subjects. How are they treated, and in what ways have the authors succeeded in finding, or failed to find, the right "level" and tone of voice. Look, also, at the size, layout, and use of illustration in modern nonfiction. Decide what makes your own book different and your own perspectives on the subject fresh. When you feel confident in your choice of subject, you may produce a more convincing text or synopsis.

Nonfiction is an expensive, cutthroat, and quickly "disposable" market. Material is updated all the time, and any publisher willing to risk a new author is likely to be more receptive if you show that you have investigated what's already available and that you understand something about children and the way *they* see their world.

Science is fun in Usborne's Science Tricks and Magic, *presented in a comic-strip form with amusing characters and bright, bold illustration.*

103

THE LEARNING EXPERIENCE

Whatever you write, it is always vital to know something about your readership and the purpose to which your writing will be put.

Living is a learning experience for children. The learning rate in early years, as they acquire language and controlled movement, is rarely equaled in intensity and pleasure in later life – in spite of all the formal structures we provide for children in the name of education. The most effective learning happens in a sequence:

1. Investigation

2. Discovery

3. Trying out and testing

4. Working out a hypothesis

5. Refining

6. Absorbing and putting into action

The learning sequence is an *active* process, which includes some time for reflection to shape and test whatever the *activity* has inspired.

For children this process can happen anywhere, but it is stimulated by activities connected with home, with friends of a similar age, with school or through the media. The learning that becomes internalized as part of personal experience comes largely from the first three sources (home, friends and school), where a child is actively engaged in asking questions, responding to answers and working out how these fit with experience. The best examples of media-stimulated learning therefore are those that offer active involvement, to capitalize on the learning style of most children.

Until the experience of school, what a child learns takes place within the context of the home and with friends. It involves the child in gaining greater control of personal action and speech through lots of watching, imitation and repetitive playful practice. This leads to greater personal responsibility, as a result of increased individual autonomy.

Two of the most important things to remember in writing nonfiction for children are

Helen Oxenbury builds her story of Helping *around the daily life of a toddler, giving the youngest children a familiar way into the world of fact.*

where and how children learn. Something else to recognize is that children naturally weave stories around events in their lives, so that for the youngest children there may be no need to create a strong distinction between writing styles used for fact or fiction. Stories of fact and fantasy both stimulate their imaginations. John Burningham and Helen Oxenbury have captured the importance of learning through everyday experience in their books for very young children. Their books assume the investigation, discovery and testing that is a familiar part of every young child's life but the record of such an experience in a book provides a new point of reference for thinking. A child looking at the pictures knows what is going on, even if the circumstances are unfamiliar, so that new ideas are provoked about something that may have been taken for granted.

The "What if . . ." type of question can stimulate greater understanding and also generate yet more questions. The good book can offer one answer but also suggest many alternatives. A nonfiction book for children succeeds best when it accepts these parameters – that it offers

Hippos at Home, *written by Althea and illustrated by Bettina Paterson, combines solid information and an enjoyable narrative.*

THE CHILD'S PERSPECTIVE

How might a child see the world? From my experience as a teacher of 5 to 12 year-olds, I would suggest that:

- A child's world is full of "now," which needs dealing with.

- The scale of a child's world is bigger and more oppressive than it seems to an adult.

- A child's world is full of specific experiences – children need lots of these before any generalization is meaningful.

- A child's world is full of incomprehensible delays and restraints.

- A child's world is full of momentous decisions.

- A child's world is very energetic.

- A child's world is today, tomorrow and yesterday.

- A child's world is full of feeling.

- A child's world is full of people who know everything that he or she doesn't.

one perspective (the author's) but provokes more questions.

Adults tend to have a very conservative and linear view about how to handle information. Children need to know things *now.* When something is important, they need to have their excitement matched by stimulating resource material that they can make sense of.

Many information books offer a world of answers or a body of irrefutable knowledge. Such books have an exclusive, authoritarian voice that can make a child reader feel rather distanced – when, having sought reassurance and information in a familiar area, the child's own experience is rarely drawn upon to illuminate a new or difficult concept.

RESEARCHING TOGETHER

As a writer, it is essential that you keep the partnership between your young readers and the publisher at the heart of what you do. With the potential partnership between yourself and a likely publisher in mind, you need to consider whether your idea is ephemeral – responding only to an immediate need in the market – or longer lasting, covering general principles. It may affect the way you tackle the necessary research.

How to find the facts . . .

Sketch out for yourself the scope of the text areas you think it important to touch on. It may be helpful to spread these thoughts randomly over a sheet of plain paper. Then, using each thought as a "hub," draw spokes outward on which to connect further thoughts as they occur to you. You then have several "wheels of action." Now list on your "wheels of action" any information that may need to be gleaned

from interviews with large organizations or institutions. You will need to create a schedule for yourself since you must offer anyone providing you with information adequate time to respond. A month to six weeks is not unreasonable, because you may be dealing with individuals whose calendars are filled months ahead or whose departments may be hard-pressed, or you may be approaching organizations in which relevant departments may be inundated with unsolicited requests for data. Some of the people you contact now may become very important as your book progresses. Get in touch with them as soon as you can – preferably by letter. Outline your needs, and your timetable and find out if they are

Below *This Longman's children's atlas packs a great deal of information into a limited area.* **Right** *A wheel of action showing how one idea can trigger others.*

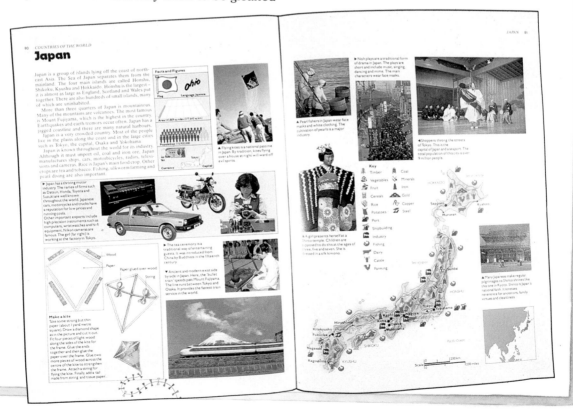

WHEEL OF ACTION

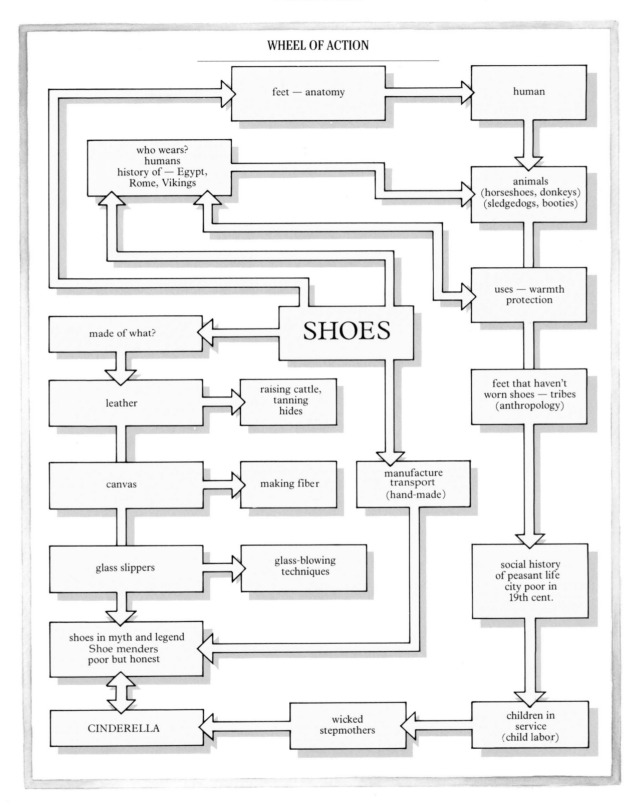

A SAMPLE SYNOPSIS

This synopsis for a book about film shows the author's reworkings.

THE MOVIES: A SYNOPSIS

4-5 Notes on invention of the cinema. First film shown by Lumiere brothers, reaction of audience, what that first film was about.

6-7, 8-9 The discovery of film - ie photographs taken to find out how many feet a galloping horse has on the ground. To lead on to explanation of flip cartoons, zoetropes, magic lanterns, simple cameras ①

10-11 TV multiple screen drive-ins; US takes over film industry from France; invention of sound ② the "talkies."

12-13 Responsibilties of continuity section/props/art director ③

14-15 Detail of a modern movie camera. ④ Use cut-away diagram. Role of cameraman.

16-17 Early H'wood transition from silent to talkies to color. Mention of Louis B Mayer, Goldwyn. Explore old studio system ⑤

18-19 Some hints about film acting - it's not as easy as it looks ⑥

20-22 Early animation. How a cartoon is made. Some notes on Walt Disney.

23 Make your own cartoon. Explain how to make an "animated" cartoon using the minimum of props.

24--25 A breakdown of the role of producer and director ⑦

26-27 Script development/budget. Experience of writer on films like Heaven's Gate which toppled Universal due to its enormous debts after going so much over budget. ⑧

28-29, 30-31 Detailed analysis of what happens on location. Lighting, clapper loader's job. ⑨

32-33 Star system/child stars/matinee idols etc. ⑩

34-35 Special effects - mention to be made of ET, Close Encounters. ⑪

36-37-38-39 A lightning tour through film's history- looking at landmarks in cinema, different methods of production, influences, writers in H'wood.

40-41 Great film gaffes - where the continuity people fail.

42-43 Promotion and distribution of film.

44-46 Amazing film facts - three pages of the remarkable, the quirky, the breathtaking and bizarre. Facts and figures, some emphasis on humour. ⑫

47-48 Index

① Perhaps this should take up another spread. Rather than go into longwinded explanation will use illustrations with annotation and caption.

② Take invention of sound back to previous spread. This unit to concentrate on types of cinema

③ Take in director and producer spread. Will also mention role of editor.

④ Take in to after spread 8-9

⑤ Take in to after spread 10-11

⑥ Cut this? Use space to explore role of make-up and costume departments

⑦ Insert the role of editor and take back to after spread 12-13.

⑧ Probably lose this unlikely to interest children

⑨ Might be nice to render this as a day in the life- perhaps entered in the form of an hourly log.

⑩ Will make this as relevant as possible to younger readers

⑪ Also mention Star Wars.

⑫ Cut to one spread. Use single page as a glossary. Insert list of useful addresses able, and willing, to help. Having organized this, complete your schedule with library research where necessary.

As with shooting a film, it is unnecessary to tackle your research in the order in which it will be used in the final text. You can push ahead on all fronts. If you appear to reach a dead end on one line of inquiry, your "wheels of action" will provide the inspiration for others. There may be several other areas of research that can be satisfactorily dealt with while you look for new "leads" to the central mystery. Good research is like good detective work – everything and anything can be useful when looking for "clues." But try not to get sidetracked. Research can take up a lot of pleasantly spent time, but leave less time for meeting deadlines.

Researching with children

If you are unfamiliar with the age group for which you are proposing to write, approach the principal of two or three schools in different areas so as to obtain a spectrum of child response. Ask if you can work with a small group of children, say, a maximum of six youngsters. Be clear about what you want their views on. Children will need to get to know you a little before they respond in a way that will be helpful to you, so be prepared to invest some time in allowing them to tell you things about themselves too. When everyone has relaxed, ask questions in a way that lets the group give opinions rather than provoking one-word answers.

When using children's views at the research stage, it is most important to *listen* to what they think they need, then check out whether it is an approach that has, in fact, been used by other authors. It may turn out that the children's reaction is because the school doesn't have such texts in its collection! Watch children using books. Is there a particular format which is appealing, accessible and appropriate to your topic? For example, *The Human Body* by Dr Jonathan Miller and David Pelham used advanced paper-engineering techniques to convey to children how their bodies operate. The pop-up devices explain information far more graphically than any amount of text, diagram and photograph could ever hope to do. Research is not only about gathering material, it is also about gathering ideas on how to make the text accessible and salable – essential, if you are to get your work published.

The techniques of pop-up picture books were used to excellent effect in The Car, *packaged by Sadie Fields.*

Lift the flaps and you will be able to see where each part of a car belongs. The engine, gearbox, transmission, steering system (left-hand drive but in some countries right-hand drive), brakes, fuel system and suspension are all clearly illustrated in the multi-layered picture. Try and identify each part yourself.

Note
The car in this book is a small front-wheel drive saloon. It is not intended to represent a model in production, but is similar in design to a wide range of small cars.

COMPILING THE MATERIAL

The task of bringing together all your researched material in order to create the first draft text is probably the most daunting. *Everything* seems indispensable. Here your "wheels of action" chart may be helpful in finding your way through the morass. By applying certain criteria to each chunk of material, you should be able to whittle away the completely irrelevant, and linking points will emerge that will steer you toward the overall organization of the final text.

If working in partnership with an illustrator or photographers it may be helpful at this stage to select appropriate supporting material and decide upon its relative importance within the text. If not, and this is more usual, make notes as you go along of possible illustrations, photographs or diagrams which will help to illuminate your text. Make detailed notes of likely sources – the more unusual the better – and provide, where possible, good roughs for material to be illustrated.

It may be necessary for you to work at two levels: a skeletal text set out as picture captions while at the same time elaborating the subject in the main text. This is a fairly standard technique in children's nonfiction because it stimulates a young confident reader to try the text, secure in the knowledge that she or he can rely on illustration and caption when the main text becomes difficult. Such a text also supports and encourages the less confident reader to "read" at a less difficult level of intellectual interest (via the captions) without emphasizing the inherent defeat of the longer text.

Keeping your audience and format in mind as you draft is vital if you are going to get as much value into limited text space as you can. Try to maintain a sense of the whole book as you write and aim to complete a first draft of the complete text before going back over it.

When you have completed your first draft, read everything through from the beginning.

Right *Photographs can bring the subject nearer to the child's experience although an artist's recreation is sometimes vital for an understanding of the past.*

MANAGING YOUR MATERIAL
A FIVE-POINT PLAN FOR SUCCESS

1. Remember the market – accurate, attractive, accessible, up-to-the-minute information is required.

2. Use firsthand sources. Be wary about quoting from previously published texts – you may infringe an author's copyright by doing so. Make sure any quotes are clearly identified. Check with your publisher about permissions and payments needed for the use of copyright material.

3. Be clear about fact and opinion. Children are just as susceptible as adults to assumptions of fact on the basis of opinion. In organizing the material, offer both, but make the distinction clear and stimulate the reader to make up his or her own mind.

4. Play your strengths. When you have pared your source material down to a manageable level, attempt your first draft in the areas where you feel most confident. As you begin work, the flow of writing will help you through the less easy sections.

5. Children are learners in the art of reading as well as in your subject matter. If the way you convey your idea is too complex, the young reader will not be able to get past the words to the meaning. Keep it simple.

The Golden Age

The Great Clippers

The first true clipper, the US *Ann McKim*, built in Baltimore in 1832, was then the fastest thing afloat. British owners, anxious to keep the tea trade from China and India, followed the American example. The *Sir Lancelot* of 1865 could sail from Foochow, China, to the Lizard in Cornwall, England, in 85 days. But in 1869, America's first coast-to-coast railroad and the Suez Canal were both opened. One doomed round-the-Horn clipper trade. The other handed tea to the steamship. The clippers' brief glory was soon to be over.

The Parts of a Clipper Ship

The Spars This ship has three masts: **fore**, **main** and **mizzen**. Each mast is made of three parts: **lower**, **top** and above **top gallant** and **royal** all in one (sometimes two pieces). Between lower mast and topmast is a platform or **top**. Between topmast and topgallant is a **crosstree**. Slung across the masts are **yards** from which square sails hang. On lower mainmast and lower mizzenmast is a **gaff** at the top and a **boom** at the bottom, holding between them fore and aft sails. At the bow a short **bowsprit** has a longer **jib-boom** above it.

The Sails On the jib-boom: 1. **fore topmast staysail** 2.**jib** 3.**flying jib** On the foremast: 4.**foresail** or **fore course** 5.**fore lower topsail** 6.**fore upper course** 7.**fore topgallant** 8.**fore**...

The pencils are put into boxes of each colour, ready to be packed. They are packed in an order which was decided upon after asking lots of people for their preferences.

Would you choose the same order if it were up to you? Give ten pencils to some friends and see how their choices differ.

A square of plastic is slid over the pencils and the packer turns down the edges of the pack to hold the crayons in place. The pack of pencils is complete.

The pencils are always packed with the colours in the same order

The pack of coloured pencils is now ready to be sent to the shops for you to buy.

28

TESTING YOURSELF

When you have an organized draft text, then go back and test it against your first principles:

- Is it honest about ambivalence between fact and opinion?
- Does it engage the reader's personal experience?
- Does the language explain a new concept clearly?
- Does the organization of the material lead the reader toward new discoveries and conclusions?
- Do the proposed pictures relate clearly to the text?
- Does it stimulate further inquiry?
- Are there many elements that may date the book too quickly?
- If the text is responding to an immediate need for information on a new subject, is the data as up-to-date as possible?

Once you have confidently tackled these issues you are ready to test the text with experts and your potential readership.

The shape of the book should begin to emerge. You may be surprised to find that sections you were convinced should bear a particular relationship to one another will work out in a different, but still well-suited, order. Some people find that working with a word processor at this stage can be invaluable, since there is much juggling of text to be done – editing, expanding and re-ordering.

TESTING AND RESHAPING THE TEXT

Being dispassionate about your creation can be painful and difficult if you have never experienced others being critical of your output or ideas. But textual criticism is essential if your proposed book is to be of the highest possible quality. If you enlisted the help of specialist advisers, institutions or groups in the course of your research, they must be sent a copy of the whole text to see how they, and the information they provided, have been represented in context. It may also be helpful to go back to your group of children at this stage to check their response. Structuring a session so that you both have a constructive experience is not always easy, but common sense and some basic principles should help you to achieve a worthwhile result.

- Work with up to six children who have some knowledge and interest in what you are doing.

- Identify specific things you want to test, such as difficult language, complex layout or unclear organization.

- Make sure you have enough clearly legible copies of the material if you want them to respond directly to the text.

- Identify some tasks for pairs of children to tackle, which will confront them with those things that you need to test.

- Make sure you have adequate means of recording their oral responses such as a tape recorder.

Listen and watch while children are giving feedback. Don't ask questions; the text should be a sufficient guide. If children need support to understand it, you will need to revise your text accordingly.

When you have received your "expert" feedback it can be helpful to let the text and

---

GOALS

Your completed text should aim to:

- Challenge the reader – slightly beyond his or her normal range of understanding.

- Indicate channels of further investigation and a structure for investigation where appropriate.

- Provide reference sources where valuable and appropriate.

- Support specialist language with a glossary.

- Ensure that contents, index pages, references and glossary interrelate accurately.

---

the criticism lie dormant for at least a day or two so that you can approach revision with a more dispassionate eye. Tackle general points of style and format first. This may help you to keep the text in perspective. More detailed alterations should then fit easily into your final structure. You may want to retest your former areas of difficulty with the children who helped you to identify them to see whether you have resolved the problem. Having done so, you can now write your final text.

By this stage you are ready to send copies of your text to publishers whom your research has indicated might be appropriate (see *Appendix*, page 138). Always keep a master copy of your text for yourself. Publishers are very busy and if your text is not suited to their list they are likely to send you a standard rejection letter when they return your manuscript.

If, however, they feel the general nature of the book fits their market, they may ask you to rework elements of your text with a particular emphasis. They will want to see your reworked text before committing themselves further: some authors may not be capable of making the adjustments required!

Should you be fortunate enough to have your text accepted, further editorial refinements and photographic or graphic elements may need to be added before the book meets the high standards required of contemporary nonfiction production. The publisher will probably want to discuss the illustration suggestions you have made, but will be ultimately responsible for commissioning photographs and other illustrative material within a production budget.

The use of diagrams can make difficult material accessible and interesting.

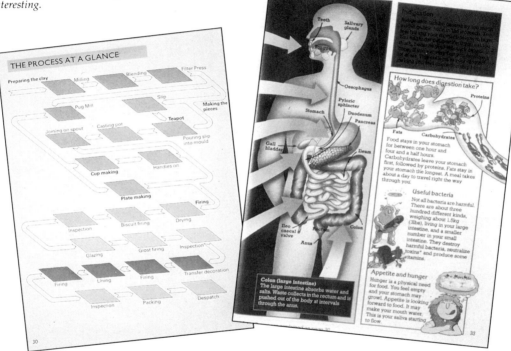

CONCLUSION

If the qualities outlined in this chapter are integral to your text, then the result will be one of those rare books which encourages children to take a leap down the road of learning. Children absorb a lot about form and structure as they read a good quality book. They may not be able to analyze why it is good or why they recognize that it works, but they know it does, and the way they approach a task afterwards reflects it.

A book can be crucial in a child's learning. It can be a catalyst or it can be an irrelevant blind alley. Sadly, the style of many nonfiction books has resulted in the latter experience rather than the former because authors and publishers have omitted the vital link in the partnership in their work – the audience! Nowadays the nonfiction book is no longer seen as an end in itself, but rather as a step on the way to learning more. The way in which it achieves this is limited only by the imagination of the author and the budget and commitment of the publisher!

Chapter 8

Fad Books

To many people a children's book is still a cover wrapped around 160 pages of paper and print, either fiction or fact, occasionally enlivened with photographs and/or drawings, or a flat 32-page book with brightly colored illustrations and minimal text.

Dismiss such ideas from your mind. Nowadays a book can be almost anything within covers that can persuade children that reading is one of life's more pleasant and rewarding occupations. The range of material that is currently produced by publishers is staggering. These exciting and appealing and certainly very different books are often (somewhat dismissively) called "fad books."

What is a fad book? The *Oxford English Dictionary* defines "fad" as "to be busy about trifles" – and that is an almost perfect description. A trifle that amuses: joke books; pop-up books; flap books; books on wheels; books with pockets; soft books; block books; shaped books; books with slots and cutouts; books in which you stick your own pictures; scratch and sniff books; carousel books; books that turn into board games; jigsaw books; push-out books; bathtub books; tactile books where parts of the pictures appear when you press your hand on the page; coloring books; quiz books; dot-to-dot books; books that glow in the dark; books with holograms; books that feature a favorite toy or TV character; books about pop groups; computer books; books that play music; and perhaps the greatest success story of recent years – interruptive fiction.

Fad books are essentially ephemeral

my red wellies

my cold ice-cream

my fluffy rabbit

Below *Janet and Allan Ahlberg have created lots of appealing picture books for young children, many with interesting graphic devices.* The Jolly Postman, *full of things for the child to discover and use over and over again, is their most unusual book to date.*

So Goldilocks put the pound note
In the pocket of her frock,
A... ...e Postman joined the party
... all played 'Postman's Knock'.

Below *Rod Campbell delights in the "toy book" form. His* Favorite Things *is a simple idea for the very young child: a cut-out zigzag book which helps the child to recognize the shape of an object as well as its image.*

my woolly hat

my green balloon

my piece of cake

rather than works of literary merit, but they should not be totally discounted. They can develop many skills apart from the skill of reading, and they are invaluable in attracting even non-reading children to the *idea* of books as a pleasant way to use their leisure time; they dispel the idea that "books = school = work." Fad books are therefore an important part of a child's learning experience. There must be hundreds of parents who have waited for what seemed to be forever to see their child show even a faint glimmer of interest in books, and who have greeted with joy the sight and sound of *1000 Worst Jokes* at the bedside or even dinner table! It can so often be the first step on the path to reading.

The decade 1975 to 1985 must have given any observer of publishing the impression that the industry was striving to become more relevant to the conditions of the marketplace. It was time for a desperately needed injection of excitement. Publishers looked at the success of the toy industry and took a few ideas from it. The influence of the toy trade on books has been, and continues to be, enormous, and during this period, if a book didn't pop up, have flaps, slots, stickers or a choice of endings, it struggled to find a place. But sales proved that the industry was right to follow this path.

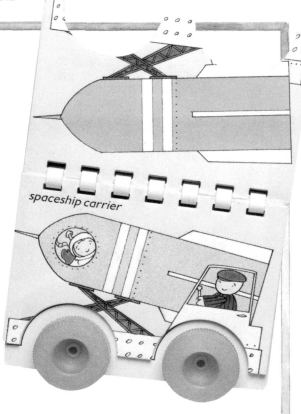

Rod Campbell's Wheels *come in both large and miniature sized books for different sized hands. Is it a toy? Is it a book? It's both!*

EARLY NOVELTY BOOKS

Fad books are not a new phenomenon thought up during the latter part of the 20th century. The first *movable* books were published in 1760. John Newbury's Harlequin books, which were turn-up books rather than pop-up books, were followed in the early part of the 19th century by "Juvenile Drama Panoramas." But the real publishing of movable books began with Dean & Son, which, from the 19th century onward, published all sorts of movable books from dissolving pictures to peepshow books. Dean had a virtual monopoly on novelty books until German publishers appeared on the scene and used the paper itself to pop up as the reader turned the pages.

Summer Surprises, published in 1896, was 1in thick when closed, and when it opened each scene had a depth of about 3ft!

The most famous author/producers of novelty books in the late 19th century were Ernest Nister and Lothar Meggendorfer. Nister perfected the art of the dissolving picture – that is, pictures printed on slats that slide over each other – and Meggendorfer was a skilled engineer. He used interconnected cardboard levers between each picture and its backing to make the pictures move (not unlike the method used today).

Meggendorfer's books are beautiful and intricate. *International Circus*, published in

1888, was made up of an unfolding panorama of six circus rings. Each ring had four layers of three-dimensional scenery and performers, and the audience consisted of 450 individually painted people. Both Nister's and Meggendorfer's books are genuine works of art. Maybe a hundred years from now someone will be saying the same about the novelty books we produce today, but mass-production techniques may preclude this.

Novelty and pop-up books continued to be popular right up to the beginning of World War I when, because most of the books were produced in Germany, the supply virtually dried up. In fact, between World War II and the 1970s hardly anything was produced in this area. It was only the toy companies, and later the greeting-card manufacturers, that kept pop-ups alive.

In the 1950s two *Winnie-the-Pooh* pop-ups were produced by Methuen in London; a few "cheap-and-nasties" also appeared at that time, but on the whole the pop-up was a rarity. The real burgeoning came in the 1970s, spearheaded by *The Many Mice of Mr Grice*, published by Random House in New York in 1974, and followed by *The Most Amazing Hide-and-Seek Alphabet Book* by Robert Crowther, published by Kestrel (now Viking) in London in 1977. Its success was phenomenal, and it opened the floodgates.

The 19th-century book producer, Lothar Meggendorfer, invented "paper engineering." This is a scene from The Doll's House.

Robert Crowther had produced his alphabet as his final year project at art school. He had figured out the paper engineering himself, even though it was not his specialty, and sent his project along to Puffin on the advice of a printer. It obviously had to be produced in hardback, and was subsequently published by Kestrel. But so little was known about producing pop-ups in the UK that the production manager finally contacted Hallmark Cards, which recommended a printer in Colombia that produced all its pop-up greeting cards. The engineering was modified slightly at its request, and the book finally produced. The first UK print run was an almost unheard-of 50,000 copies.

(Later, when Wally Hunt of Intervisual Communications, the undisputed "King" of the pop-up, who has produced virtually all the pop-up books presently on the market and who controls the production companies in Colombia and Hong Kong, finally saw a copy of the finished book, he said to the Kestrel people "*It's fine, but do you folks realize*

Below *Raymond Briggs'* Fungus the Bogeyman, *that marvelously irreverent poke-in-the-eye of adulthood..*

Right *An unforgettable image for Jan Pienkowski's* Haunted House.

I can't seem to settle down. In fact I can't sit still for two minutes.

that you've just reinvented the wheel? Why didn't you come to me?")

In the years that followed there was a deluge of pop-up books, each one more intricate and imaginative than its predecessor. Famous illustrators joined the throng, with Jan Pienkowski's *Haunted House* (1979) and the transfer of Raymond Briggs' enormously successful *Fungus the Bogeyman* (1982) into a pop-up version. Pop-up books became an industry in their own right.

In retrospect, Robert Crowther's book was very simple compared with later entrants to the field. The sheer tactical wizardry of later examples such as *The Facts of Life* and the application of the magic of pop-ups to factual books, for example in *The Car*, is staggering.

FROM HOLES TO "FEELIES"

Pop-ups aren't the only novelty books on the scene. In the early 1970s Dick Bruna's immensely popular ABC pull-out frieze was published, followed by many others. In fact, Dick Bruna was one of the first authors whose work was successfully merchandized, his characters appearing on a wide range of goods – from wallpaper to china.

Eric Carle's *The Very Hungry Caterpillar*, in which a caterpillar slowly eats its way through the week (and the pages of the book), came out in 1970. Ten years later

Where's Spot?, a lift-the-flap book, was published, followed by a range of Spot books, including bathtub books (screenprinted vinyl with a soft filling), which were published in 1984. *Yum-Yum*, a slot book by Janet and Allan Ahlberg, also published in 1984.

Rod Campbell, another innovative author/illustrator of books for very young children, brought toys and books even closer together with the publication of *Wheels* in 1983. (*Wheels* is a book about machines with big wheels – including trucks, buses and rocket

On Saturday he ate through one piece of chocolate cake, one ice-cream cone, one pickle, one slice of Swiss cheese, one slice of salami.

one lollipop, one piece of cherry pie, one sausage, one cupcake, and one slice of watermelon.

That night he had a stomachache.

Before going to bed, Buster washes his hands and face.

Feel the warm towel!

Top *Eric Carle's* The Very Hungry Caterpillar. **Above** Buster's Bedtime *by Rod Campbell.*

carriers – and sports a fine set itself.)

Lots of books appeared with parts that could be pushed out and made into models (e.g. *Zartax the Invincible Transrobot*) or simply dressed a character, such as Sindy or Princess Di. There were books that incorporated jigsaw puzzles, and there was *Little Choo Choo's Runaway Adventure*, which included a model train, a track *and* a pop-up.

The very first tactile book, so far as I am aware, is *Pat the Bunny*, which was first published by Golden Books, New York, in 1942!

More recently, Random House in the US and a small British firm called Red Balloon Books have led the way with tactile books such as *Soft as a Kitten* – which encouraged children to feel, touch, see and sniff – and *Toby's Day*, an imaginative little book with a zipper to undo, a quilt to feel, a mirror in which to look at yourself and a fluffy cat lying under a striped sheet – all of which you can feel and/or see.

Tactile books are beginning to have a wider application in the teaching of children with impaired vision and hearing. An early popular success was the biography of Louis Braille, which has the complete Braille alphabet imprinted on the back cover.

There were also shape books. Rod Campbell created a range of books including *My Pet* – a little cardboard book of familiar animal shapes. And anyone who remembers with affection the old cloth books will still find them, together with the newer ones that come padded with soft foam, bearing pockets in which there is a little toy that can be moved from page to page.

The latest novelties are those that incorporate pictures printed with heat-sensitive ink, where parts of the picture appear only when you apply the warmth of your hand – or inadvertently leave them on the radiator, which also does the trick! These inks have also been used for books that glow in the dark.

CHOOSE YOUR OWN ADVENTURE...

In 1979 the first interrupted-text book appeared – the forerunner of a genre of fiction that has achieved vast success. Marketed under many series names, these books have one thing in common: the text stops at strategic points for the reader to make decisions, to become the star of the story and to follow his or her own path through the text. Depending upon the decision the reader makes, the story can end in triumph or disaster. As one 10-year-old reader said: *"I was suffocated twice, buried alive once and had a spell put on me – all in one night!"*

The first *Choose Your Own Adventure*, by Edward Packard, was published by Bantam in the US in 1979 and by Corgi in the UK in 1982. The stories are not complicated and they proved to be immensely popular with the less-motivated reader. The series now numbers over 50 titles. The simple *Choose Your Own Adventure* books were swiftly followed by the slightly more sophisticated solo role-playing adventure books such as Jackson and Livingstone's Fighting Fantasy series; the first title to appear was *Warlock of Firetop Mountain*. There are now 30 titles in the series, which has chalked up sales of over 10 million copies.

Fantasy role-playing books are very big business indeed. They evolved from strategic role-play games and have developed in complexity to the current state of the art where you need two dice, three friends, and the games book to "share adventures in a magical world." As the cover blurb of one book says: *"this book gives you the essentials for combat; a complete armory and a bestiary of bloodthirsty opponents. You choose the type of warrior you want to be – an armor-clad knight, a muscle-bound Barbarian, a tough dwarf or a crafty elf. Take up your sword, your war ax or your bow. Within ten minutes you will be battling your first deadly foe in a perilous adventure. LIFE AND DEATH ARE ONLY A DICE ROLL AWAY!"* Irresistible!

Role-playing books have often succeeded where all others have failed in attracting a young teenage male readership, and many parents and teachers have commented on the fact that once they have become hooked on these books they have gone on to become readers of a wide range of material.

Of course, the books have not escaped without criticism. "Gratuitously violent," "bloodthirsty," "pandering to the baser instincts" and "stereotyping" are just a few of the remarks made about them. But where would a trend be without critics?

SPOTTING THE TRENDS

No article about fad books could ignore those that appear and almost immediately disappear, like the scores of books that were published about BMX bikes and skateboards. The publisher has to act very fast to get a book on the market before the trend wanes and the rewards go to those who are brave enough to take their chances on a trend happening.

JOKE BOOKS

There *is* one kind of fad book that will never let you down, and that is the joke book. There are hundreds of joke books on the market, but there is always room for more. Find a theme, gear your jokes around it, and you are away.

Hands up those who remember elephant-joke fever and the tidal wave of knock-knocks? Everybody wants to be able to tell a good joke, and children are no exception.

STICKER BOOKS

Another great favorite is the sticker book. Not the kind of sticker books you can buy at stationery stores and fill with pictures of baseball players sold in packets, but books in which reusable vinyl stickers are an integral part, from Hippo's very simple *Hide and Seek Sticker Mysteries* to the fascinating book *Dinosaurs*, published by Macdonald. These books are far removed from early sticker books in which the stickers were like postage stamps and, once stuck down, were there for eternity. We are only beginning to explore the possibilities of working with vinyl stickers, and it will be fascinating to see how they develop.

POP BOOKS AND TIE-INS

Pop books, film tie-ins and TV-related books are also considered to be fad books. Pop books range from pop quiz books, to books for fans of the "fanzine" type, to in-depth examinations of a particular pop group or rock star.

Above all, pop books demand perfect timing and superb photographs, and knowledgeable authors and publishers. Pop stars can disappear faster than snow in summer!

Nothing emphasizes the transitory nature of a fad book more clearly than the decline in sales of the movie tie-in. There was a time when publishers would practically kill for the new movie books, and at its peak the picture storybook of the movie would sell in millions. *ET* was probably the last of the mega-sellers, although, as recently as 1985, *Ghostbusters* sold very well worldwide, and even more recently *Karate Kid II* has proved popular enough to persuade the producers to go ahead with *Karate Kid III* and the licensing of a toy company to produce a range of karate figures. The change in the way people spend their leisure time is reflected in the figures produced for the number of video hirings and sales for the Karate Kid movies, and the not overly impressive box office receipts.

This is borne out by the relative strength of television-related books and merchandise. For many years there has been a strong market for TV-related books. Although the target age of the viewers is preschool, it extends very much farther, and the really big children's TV characters have countless fans. You need look no further for proof than the personals that can be found in the newpapers on Valentine's Day. The two new contenders for the title of "classic" are *Spot* and probably, *The Shoe People.* *Spot*, like *Thomas the Tank Engine*, is book-based; *The Shoe People* were created with television in mind, and already, before a single episode has been shown, there is an extensive book and licensing program in existence.

TV programs aimed at an older age group have a much shorter life, and their audience is obviously more fickle. The A-Team, Knight Rider, Street Hawk, EastEnders, Roland Rat, Dempsey and Makepeace and Miami Vice have all had their time in the sun, although Miami Vice is the only program I know that has spawned a juvenile spoof – *Miami Mice*, published in 1986.

LICENSED CHARACTERS

TV-related characters lead almost inevitably to licensed characters – the other major force of the last few years. Like fad books, licensed characters have been with us for some time. The oldest character of all is Walt Disney's Mickey Mouse; the most famous is probably Charles Schulz's Snoopy and the whole Peanuts gang; the biggest, recently, is My Little Pony, with a reported five million books sold on the back of the toys. Almost anything *could* be licensed, but in practice the characters come mainly from TV and the toy companies. The range of toys available for licensing is enormous. The current crop includes My Little Pony – still a favorite; Care Bears; Gummi Bears; the Wuzzles; He-Man and She-Ra; Barbi; Sindy; Jem; Muppet babies; Pound puppies; Wrinkles; Cabbage Patch Dolls; Moondreamers; Transformers; Mask; Centurions; Defenders of the Earth; Teddy Ruxpin (the teddy bear with the tape recorder in its stomach); and Visionaries – Knights of the Magical Light and their adversaries, the Darkling Lords, all of which incorporate holograms. Some will develop and become well-loved characters in their own right, while others will disappear quietly. The strength of a good character is in the range it can offer –

from the main toy to all the accessories to go with it. Publishing plays a very important part in establishing a character, with coloring books, activity books, sticker books and reading books adding to the range of "collectables."

The licensor (the toy company or its licensing agent) will provide tremendous backup to the publisher by providing story lines, character outlines, artwork styles and even the colors to be used in printing to produce an image consistent with the toy or character. But again, if by using a favorite character or toy one can encourage children to read, that is justification enough.

Publishing has become much more innovative in the last decade, and looking back one wonders if any stone has been left unturned! But authors and illustrators are infinitely inventive, and publishers have become increasingly adventurous and are always prepared to consider new and revolutionary ideas. At the end of the day we are all fighting for a share of children's leisure time and money. Books have never had a particularly glamorous image, but fad books are providing this. They bring a bit of showbiz into books for the young.

FINDING YOUR WAY IN

So how do you break into the golden circle of fad-book creators?

If you have a wonderful idea, check the market carefully before you approach a publisher; your revolutionary idea may be a rehash of someone else's brainwave, and there may already be something similar in the stores.

Present your ideas as lucidly as possible and explain why your approach to a subject is genuinely different.

Try to fit your idea to the right publisher: if you have come up with the ultimate joke book find out who publishes the sort of joke book you like and try your idea on them.

Series are often written by more than one

person – the originator of the idea and one or two others who can match the original author's style. If there is a series you would love to contribute to, try your hand at a specimen and see if you can do it. Analyze the plots and construction and try to discover what the differences are between the most and least successful titles in the series. If you are happy with your work sound out the publisher for a reaction. It may be that, even if you don't end up writing for the original series, the publisher will try you out for something different.

But don't get disheartened. In publishing, more than any other trade, one man's meat is another man's poison!

Chapter 9

The Hopeful Author – Getting Your Work Published

 Every day, hopeful authors parcel up their work and commit their precious manuscripts, via the mail, to the unknown. For most people, it's like sending their baby off alone across a stormy sea. Will the boat be lost without trace? Will it be wrecked on some wholly unforeseen hazard? Or will the voyage end happily with the precious burden appearing as a shiny new book temptingly offered on a publisher's list? And every day, editors receive multitudinous offerings, often accompanied by letters that indicate that the hopeful authors really have no idea what they are doing.

Sadly it isn't possible to acquire genius – or even talent – from a book. There are, though, plenty of things a first-time author can do to help himself or herself in the quest for a publisher. Some are dictated by common sense; some might require a little research on the part of the would-be writer. There are also technical matters of which the beginner may have vaguely heard. Some explanations may help to allay anxieties about these dimly perceived mysteries. The person who works through the following pages will, it is hoped, end up with a better understanding of what to do and why.

FINDING THE RIGHT PUBLISHER
"Flotsam and Jetsam Marine Books…"

One of the most basic mistakes made by a beginner is to send his or her work to the wrong place! At the simplest level, check that the address you have found is reasonably up-to-date. Publishers *do* move offices, and the address on the copyright page of a 20-year-old book may not now be correct. Publishers are listed in the directories *The Literary Market Place*, *Writer's Market,* and *Artist's Market*, all of which can be found at your local library (see *Appendix,* page 138). The telephone directory is another useful source of information. If you have the name of a publisher that does not appear in any of these places, it may have gone out of business or been taken over.

If a reasonable hunt turns up nothing, try another company.

The second basic mistake is to send the manuscript to the wrong kind of publisher! A little thought by the letter-writer (*opposite page*) might have led him to the reasonable conclusion that the publisher (an invented house) might not take children's books and consulting one of the directories would have confirmed this, because each publisher's areas of interest are comprehensively listed.

Having established that the publisher actually *does* publish children's books, the next thing to find out is whether the publisher

Flotsam and Jetsam Marine Books
25 West 26th Street
New York
New York 10012

Dear editor,

I have written a novel for children aged 6-19, entitled The Hopeful
Writer. It's a historical fantasy in verse, and the hero is a pig
who plays baseball. The MS is   500 pages long, and is
handwritten. I have read it to the children in school, who loved it
nd said it ought to be published.

Sadly I cannot find an illustrator, but I envisage the book having
pictures in full color throughout. I would like to have it published in time for Christmas.

I think I need an gent since I understand publishers never take
books from authors they don't know. Could you tell me how to get
one? I am reluctant to show you the complete ms since I don't want
my brilliant idea to be taken by anyone else. How can I protect
my copyright? I am enclosing some random pages for you to read.
Please let me know by retrun about a contract. I have approached
several other publishers as well as you.

Yours sincerely,

Ethan Chapin

My address is
73 County Ridge Drive
Raleigh
North Carolina

---

72 Meadowbank Road
Raleigh
North Carolina
27609

The Children's Editor
Goodbook Publishing
Woodcliffe Lake Drive
Secacaus
New Jersey
07094

Dear Sir

With this letter I enclose my picturebook text/children's novel/
non-fiction text entitled THE HOPEFUL WRITER.

I would be most grateful if you would consider it for publication,
but I have enclosed a stamped self-addressed envelope for its
return should it prove to be unsuitable.

I shall look forward to hearing from you in due course.

Yours faithfully

Fiona Neale

Above *How not to address yourself to a publishing house.* **Right** *The right way to go about it — a short, straightforward covering note, cleanly typed and well set out.*

takes books like yours! A firm that specializes in books for older teenagers may not be able to tackle a picture book and will have to turn it down. On the other hand, a firm that has a strong line in animal stories may not be able to cope with science fiction! In either case – failing to identify a children's publisher *or* failing to identify the nature of his list – the hopeful author will get a letter of rejection, which can be avoided by a little homework.

It also helps to check your local public library and bookstores. The publisher's name is usually fairly prominently displayed on the title page and spine of a book, but it will also appear on the biblio or copyright page – usually immediately after the title page. If the book is a paperback, find the line that says, "First published by . . . ." This will tell you which company first published the book, and that's the firm you should approach. It should be possible to find out quite quickly, by examining books that appear to be roughly similar to your own, which firms have published in the area you're interested in: whether it is for a younger or older readership, a picture book, family adventure, animal story, highly illustrated nonfiction or narrative nonfiction. Doing this kind of research won't make the quest 100 per cent foolproof – your chosen publishing house might have just made a policy decision not to publish that kind of children's book – but it will considerably reduce the risk of rejection.

And remember – it's still true that most picture books, novels and nonfiction are published in hardback first, and that later on a paperback publisher may buy the right to reprint it in a paperback edition. Original paperbacks generally fall into very specific categories – for example, film and TV tie-ins, books about the latest craze (published to catch an ephemeral interest), books to play with (the choose-your-own-adventure style), and series publishing, such as teenage romances.

So, having done your research and found that the publisher still exists, that you have a reasonably recent address and that the firm has a list of children's books which includes examples of the sort of book you have in mind – what next?

FINDING YOUR AUDIENCE
"…a novel for children aged 6-16…"

Can you remember your own childhood? Do you have children of your own or children close at hand to study? If so, you'll remember, or notice, that the abilities and interests of someone aged six are somewhat different from those of someone aged 16. For six-year-olds, school is new and most children are still learning to read fluently. A book with chapters is something of an adventure. Reading should be fun, but it's hard work, too. By the time they are 16, *most* children, one hopes, will be reading fluently. They will know much more of the world and will be making their own decisions about courses to choose and college applications.

There is more change and diversity in a child's first 16 years than that child may experience during the whole of the rest of his or her life! That range is reflected in the children's book industry.

It's not just a question of what subjects to choose, though they are important – six-year-olds can usually manage stories about schools, families, children of their own age, animals, and mild fantasies, but are not generally geared to politics, philosophy or intricate historical argument. Sixteen-year-olds *should* be able to manage all of the latter – and many others besides – even if their favorite reading turns out to be teenage romances and books on the latest pop idol.

There are differences in the linguistic abilities of the two ages. Writing for six-year-olds mostly requires simple ideas expressed very clearly in simple words and sentence structures. And if that sounds like a recipe for boredom, it's one of the most difficult kinds of writing there is. Try it and see! Very few people can manage a picture-book text successfully. Many people, new to children's books, make the mistake of thinking "the younger, the easier." This is not true and is a great pitfall in the way of the unwary.

So however much you hope your work will appeal to a wide range of readers, don't make any extravagant claims for it! Children's book editors have a great deal of experience in judging just what age-group a particular text might suit, and on the whole it's better to leave this to them. You'd be quite correct, though, to indicate in your letter that the work was for "younger" or "older" readers!

CHOOSE YOUR SUBJECT WITH CARE

*" . . . It's a historical fantasy in verse and the hero is a pig
who plays baseball . . . "*

Publishing these days is an international business. Every editor hopes to be able to arrange as many co-editions as possible with colleagues in appropriate publishing houses around the world. When considering a picture book, it may be essential to make such sales, because color printing is horrendously expensive. The originating publisher can thus spread the cost of its edition over many thousands of copies. And, from the author's point of view, overseas sales mean extra income, which is generally interesting!

But each country in the world has different customs and habits, and a different language! Put certain elements in your book, and you may be creating problems for all concerned and cut yourself off from international co-editions. In the quoted example, there are several potential minefields.

" . . . It's historical . . . " Historical subjects are less popular now than they were a few years ago. They are harder to read, because the child must jump mentally twice: once into the story, and once into the historical period. It's mostly older girls, generally good readers, who like historical novels. Publishers will almost never take a chance on a historical novel for younger readers. And, as for overseas sales – your history could either be unknown abroad and therefore unappealing, if not a complete turn-off, or it could be offensive!

" . . . fantasy . . . " There are decided national tastes in fantasy. Some countries don't like it at all. The countries that do (both Britain and America) are well supplied with many very fine writers. Is your work fresh and different enough to stand up to massive competition? Any derivation will be spotted at once by eagle-eyed editors.

" . . . Verse . . . " Again, international problems! It doesn't translate! Most of the "poems"

that publishers are offered are actually doggerel: and, of all the things to try and write for children, poetry is probably the hardest. Sales for new poets are comparatively small, and there are only a few publishers prepared to undertake it. A new poet must be exceptionally good – fresh, vigorous, witty, with a quirky and percipient eye and ear. This is an area where even the good may be disappointed. Only the exceptional are going to reach the heights!

" . . . The hero is a pig who plays baseball . . . " Here there could be problems of too many pigs! It's surprising how often one finds that there's a glut of stories about a particular animal. If publishers are being inundated by cats or teddy bears or wombats, there simply may not be room for any more. From the outside, it may be very difficult to find this kind of thing out, but one useful rule of thumb is: if the publisher already has a successful title or series featuring an engaging puppy or a large tortoiseshell cat, don't send in yours. There won't be room on one list for the pair of them!

One general point: in picture books, animals are often dressed, either for cuteness or because the author is actually making points about people, in an appealing disguise. You may run up against an editor who is against anthropomorphism. If you do, you must simply try your work elsewhere!

" . . . Baseball . . . " This marks a text as irredeemably American! Just as doubledecker buses are irredeemably British. There are, of course, many occasions when it is quite proper, indeed necessary, to introduce national details of this sort. But *do* bear in mind that something taken for granted in one country can be quite incomprehensible in another. This is particularly important at the youngest level.

LENGTH AND PRESENTATION
" . . . the ms is 500 pages long, and is handwritten . . . "

Five hundred pages is too long! Even if your story's brilliant, any editor worth his or her salt will be reaching for the blue pencil. If you calculate 250 words on the average page, that ms will be 125,000 words long. There are no hard-and-fast rules about length, but very few children's novels today are more than 60,000 words long, and for most writers that ought to give ample scope for telling a good story. Nonfiction will generally need to be even more concise. And the younger the age for which you're writing, the shorter the text should be. Cutting text is an art every writer should practice. Read through your work and cut out anything that isn't *strictly* necessary to tell the story. This will probably include all your favorite passages! But it's necessary to be ruthless – the manuscript will be leaner, punchier and more likely to be successful.

WHY TYPE?

These days, there are very few adults who can't reach a typewriter – or, increasingly, a word processor – and it's to a writer's advantage to produce a typewritten script.

1. It's easier and faster to read. Reading literally hundreds of scripts a year, editors appreciate help, and a clean, neat, legible typewritten script is liable to be looked at with more sympathy.

2. It gives a better impression. Just as with a job application, this is important. You're selling your work, but it must speak for you without your physical presence to someone you don't know. You need to do everything you can to ensure that your work is noticed favorably. A blurred scrawl, hard to read and likely to cover the clothes and the person with ballpoint smudges, will not be greeted with enthusiasm.

3. It's cheaper! If you produce a dirty script, or a handwritten one, and the publisher does buy it, it will have to be retyped before it goes to the printer. The bill will probably be sent to you – and the publisher won't have time to shop around for a cheap typist.

4. Many publishers will refuse to read a handwritten script.

EVERYONE LOVES IT
" . . . I have read the story to children in school, who loved it
and said it ought to be published . . . "

Most editors give a hollow laugh when they read this! Most children are delighted to stop work and listen to a story – it's much more fun. They will also feel pleased and flattered if they then find out that they are the first to hear the story, or that it's been specially written for them by someone they like, so of course the author will get an enthusiastic reception. This claim, sadly, means absolutely nothing, and is no argument in favor of publication.

SETTING OUT YOUR MS

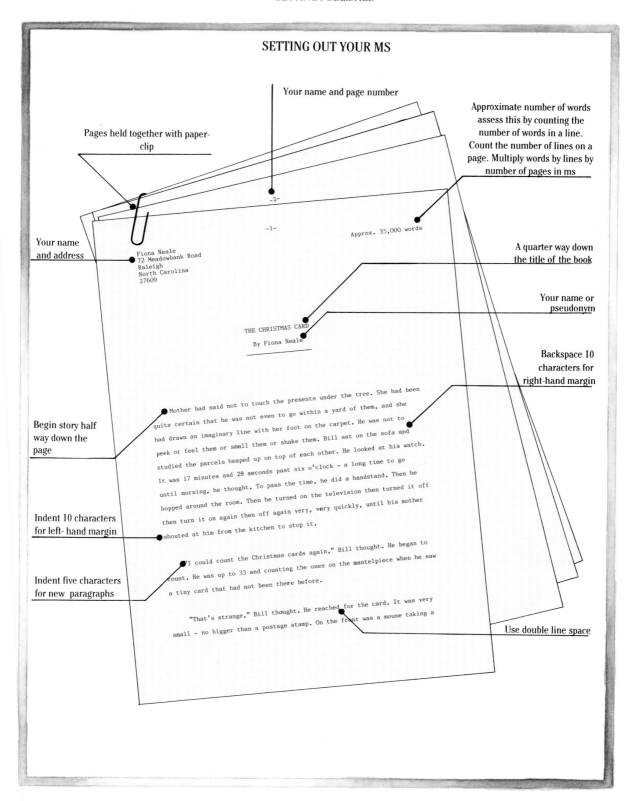

Your name and page number

Approximate number of words assess this by counting the number of words in a line. Count the number of lines on a page. Multiply words by lines by number of pages in ms

Pages held together with paper-clip

Your name and address

-2-

-1-

Approx. 35,000 words

A quarter way down the title of the book

Fiona Neale
72 Meadowbank Road
Raleigh
North Carolina
27609

Your name or pseudonym

THE CHRISTMAS CARD

By Fiona Neale

Backspace 10 characters for right-hand margin

Begin story half way down the page

Mother had said not to touch the presents under the tree. She had been quite certain that he was not even to go within a yard of them, and she had drawn an imaginary line with her foot on the carpet. He was not to peek or feel them or small them or shake them. Bill sat on the sofa and studied the parcels heaped up on top of each other. He looked at his watch. It was 17 minutes and 28 seconds past six o'clock – a long time to go until morning, he thought. To pass the time, he did a handstand. Then he hopped around the room. Then he turned on the television then turned it off then turn it on again then off again very, very quickly, until his mother shouted at him from the kitchen to stop it.

Indent 10 characters for left-hand margin

Indent five characters for new paragraphs

"I could count the Christmas cards again," Bill thought. He began to count. He was up to 33 and counting the ones on the mantelpiece when he saw a tiny card that had not been there before.

"That's strange," Bill thought. He reached for the card. It was very small – no bigger than a postage stamp. On the front was a mouse taking a

Use double line space

ILLUSTRATION

"...I cannot find an illustrator, but I envisage the book having pictures in full color throughout..."

There's no need for the author to find the illustrator. When a script is taken on, the editor – working with an art director or designer – will decide what size and shape of book is appropriate and can be afforded and what style of artwork will best suit the text. An artist can be approached who can do the right kind of pictures, to the right kind of budget and to the standard required for reproduction. For the author to try to find an artist is to walk through a minefield. The artist may impose on the book a size and shape that is quite uneconomical commercially or is not used by the publisher you have in mind. Or the artist may work in a style difficult to reproduce, or in one unsuitable for the particular text. Or, often, the artist simply may not be good enough. Far better to leave all this to your publishers who will know exactly what to look for. Of course, if you have strong ideas about pictures, you'll be able to tell your editor – once you've made your sale! If for some reason your ideas aren't feasible, a good editor should explain why.

"... Pictures in full color throughout ... " Many texts justify the expense of color printing, but often such an idea, however attractive, is completely uneconomical. In America, many picture books are still printed in only two or three colors, and in both America and Great Britain, nonfiction is frequently published with alternating color and black and white pages. Fiction almost never contains color illustration, with the exception of some large gift books – usually with texts that are out of copyright. Stories for younger readers, poetry, joke and quiz books are usually illustrated with black and white line drawings, but novels for older readers now rarely include pictures, largely because of the cost, but also because older, fluent readers are deemed not to need the help of illustrations! (See also *The Basics of Writing for Children*, page 16, *Picture Books*, page 54, *Illustration – Building a Career in Children's Books*, page 68, and *Making the Book*, page 80.)

PRESENTATION

"...I think I need an agent, since I understand publishers never take books from authors they don't know..."

Most publishers *will* take an unsolicited manuscript – provided it is good enough and fits their publishing program! But it's a long chance. One reputable publisher was producing about 12 children's novels a year – only one of which was unsolicited. That company found that hopeful authors were sending in a thousand manuscripts each year. With book sales declining or disappearing, children's lists have been cut back (fewer books are published each year) or shut down. Parent companies may have merged or been bought out, with two children's lists (or more) being combined into one new list publishing fewer books! All these things result in fewer children's lists, and fewer places to sell work!

An agent can be immensely useful to an author. A good agent will know the publishing scene backward, sideways and upside down, and will go to great lengths to place a good manuscript. Then contract negotiation and all subsequent business and financial negotiations will be undertaken for the author – allowing the writer time to get on with further work, and also (if all goes well) to develop a friendship with an editor unhindered by unseemly business considerations!

But first catch your agent! No agent will take on an author whose work he does not think he can sell or does not like. Some even

DOING YOUR RESEARCH

Do your research. Book stores and children's libraries are good places for browsing. Check what is popular at the moment; see what other authors are up to but don't plagiarize. You want to be your own first best not someone else's second best.

charge a fee for reading a manuscript. Some are reluctant to take on newcomers, preferring to represent writers with a track record: one published book is usually enough. And, of course, an agent will take a percentage of an author's earnings as a fee – usually 10 per cent of all earnings in the home market and 20 per cent overseas for literary works. It's well worth it for some. Other authors, how- ever, prefer to keep all their earnings and deal with the business aspects of publishing for themselves – and even come to enjoy it!

Lists of literary agents can be found in *Writer's Market* (see *Appendix,* page 138) and *The Literary Marketplace.*

WRITER'S PARANOIA

" . . . I am reluctant to show you the complete manuscript, because I don't want my brilliant idea to be taken by anyone else . . . "

Every children's editor has met the shy or overly wary author! But the untried author must realize that no one is going to buy goods sight unseen – an editor must be able to read a proposed text and consider it thoroughly, whatever sort of book it is. Not only is it important to see that the text is good and appropriate for the age group, but there are questions of possible derivation, plagiarism, libel and so on to be taken into account.

No reputable commercial firm is going to poach a good idea. An editor is much more likely to be delighted to have been sent an original, salable proposal and be talking about contracts. If for some reason House A cannot publish the book, it's been known for an author to be recommended to House B with happy results! Remember, too, that a well-known company has a reputation to lose and would not wish to see it damaged. If, in spite of reassurances, you are genuinely concerned for the safety of your work, it's always possible to lodge a copy with a bank or a legal representative, with a record of the date – although both banks and lawyers are liable to charge for their services!

It is only fair to point out that ideas for books – like political ideas, scientific discoveries or famines – can occur simultaneously in different places. For example, if a teacher finds the lack of a book on fruit, that teacher, with suitable qualifications, might set about writing one. But other teachers might have also noticed the lack and be writing their own books on fruit. One would not know about the others, but publishers might well be presented with the typescripts at approximately the same time. It might then happen that three different firms all announced a forthcoming title about fruit! There would have been no collusion – simply that the right cause (a lack of books on the subject) led to a similar effect (teachers who noticed and did something about it). Result – three books, which would allow other teachers quite a reasonable choice for their classrooms!

THE LAW OF COPYRIGHT FOR AUTHORS

Ideas themselves can't be copyrighted; how you express your ideas can. As soon as you write something down or draw or compose it in some tangible form, the idea in its tangible form is copyrighted and you are the holder. Although you don't need to register your copyright to have it protected, no action for infringement of copyright can be undertaken unless the copyright of a work is registered. So you can send your book to an editor for consideration without registering the copyright, then have the publisher copyright the book in your name when it is published.

When a work is published a copyright notice should appear on all copies publicly distributed. The line must include either the symbol or the word "copyright," the year of publication and the name of the copyright owner. Within three months of publication of such work, the copyright owner, or the owner of the exclusive right of publication, must deposit with the Copyright Office two complete copies of the work, for the use of the Library of Congress. Publication without a notice or with an incorrect notice won't automatically invalidate the copyright or affect the ownership; however, any error or omission should be corrected as soon as possible to prevent the eventual loss of protection.

AVOID DISAPPOINTMENT

"…I am enclosing some random pages for you to read…"

Never submit random pages from your typescript! Either send in a synopsis of your book asking whether the editor would like to read the whole text, or send in the complete manuscript. A busy editor needs to know (it cannot be repeated too often) how your story works, how you handle plot, develop characters and use dialogue. If your work is nonfiction, the same applies. The editor needs to judge how you treat your subject: in depth or superficially? Do you stimulate the reader interest, or bore him? None of these things can be judged from random pages. An editor will spend time reading a comprehensive synopsis or the complete text – but is likely to return random pages immediately as not being worth the time to read through. *Don't* run the risk of this disappointment – or indeed the waste of an envelope and stamps.

THE HOPEFUL – AND NAIVE – AUTHOR
" . . . please let me know about a contract by return mail . . . "

Well – you may discover by return mail that you *won't* get a contract. If your work is wildly unsuitable it will probably be returned at once! But generally it's unreasonable to expect an editor to reply immediately.

By now it should be clear that editors get a great number of unsolicited manuscripts. Most of them try to set aside a regular time each week for reading, and they generally read the scripts that have been waiting longest first. Reading and considering a manuscript takes time – and while many will be rejected at once (the author can't write, or the idea is stale, or it's wrong for that particular list), others may show some spark of promise. In this case the editor may want to write a detailed reply to the author, explaining exactly why it's being turned down.

WHAT YOU SHOULD DO
GETTING THE PRESENTATION RIGHT!

By now, many readers must be wondering whether they stand the remotest chance of being published, and if so, how on earth they should go about things! Your chances of being published *are* remote – you need talent and luck, and you are gambling against long odds. But for those determined enough, brave enough – or rash enough – here are the essentials.

Your manuscript

DO make sure it's typewritten.

DO use one side only of standard (8½ x 11in) paper or foolscap size paper.

DO use double line spacing.

DO leave good margins on either side of the page.

DO number pages consecutively from beginning to end of the script.

DO make sure your name and address are *on the script* – letters can get detached.

DO keep a copy of your work – publishers try not to lose things, but it can happen. The mail service has been known to lose manuscripts too!

DO write a simple, straightforward covering letter.

DO enclose postage or a stamped, addressed envelope for the return of the script.

DON'T do up the package so tightly that it can't be opened or only at the risk of gashed hands, or so carelessly that the parcel breaks and your script is lost.

DON'T – ever – if rejected, ask for detailed criticism of your work! You won't get it. Neither agent nor publisher has the time to engage in lengthy correspondence over a manuscript that for them isn't salable.

DON'T engage in long, acrimonious correspondence with editors telling them why they were wrong to reject your brilliant work – you may want to try that editor with another idea one day. Just send your script on to the next publisher on your list of possibles.

DON'T – ever – turn up on a publisher's doorstep with a script and ask to talk to someone about it ! First of all, editors will already have a busy day to get through and won't have time to fit in unscheduled appointments. Second, it's not fair to skip ahead of the line of manuscripts. Third, if your story needs explaining, it probably isn't good enough to publish. The reader has to choose the book in a store or library without you there to explain it – and the manuscript should speak for itself, too. Fourth, there is no way anyone, even a genius, could read a text of any length properly in the few moments of a meeting. Do you really want a snap judgment of your work, probably flavored with resentment because you have forced the editor to make a decision before he or she is properly ready? REMEMBER – EDITORS ARE HUMAN TOO, and have to plan their work just like anyone else. The existing system may take time, but it is designed to be as fair to everyone as possible.

Anything that's truly promising may need revisions, and again it can take time to write to the author explaining just what needs doing and why. It will also be necessary to discuss a hopeful manuscript: with other editors, with sales managers (who have to be confident that it is a book they can *sell*) and maybe with outside experts checking for accuracy or advising on educational suitability. Many houses have freelance outside readers who may write a report on an interesting text. So be prepared to be patient after submitting your work. You should get a formal acknowledgment that it has arrived; after that it can take up to two months before you hear. If, after that, there's no news, a modest inquiry about progress is in order. And no news may occasionally be good news!

"*. . . I have approached several other publishers as well as you . . .*"

Photocopying has now made it possible for an author to obtain unlimited good clean copies of a manuscript. But it's also led to a considerable increase in the number of multiple submissions made to publishers. This has become somewhat more acceptable in America than in Britain, where it is very much frowned on! The major problem is that several firms might find themselves trying to buy – or having bought – an identical script as a result of multiple submissions and the author's unfamiliarity with publishing processes. The ensuing legal tangle is fraught with difficulties – and this *has* happened. Publishers are naturally wary. You might think that simply asking the author if he has shown the work elsewhere at the same time might sort the matter out – but no! An unclear answer can be even more confusing. Some British editors also take the view that a multiple submission is an attempt by the author to force them to a faster decision – this is resented and may result in a very speedy rejection. So beware!

SYNOPSES

Some people prefer to use this form of communication. It usually results in a faster initial response from the editor, and it's cheaper for the author than sending heavy manuscripts through the mail. The drawback is that it's possible to give an inadequate résumé of your work and, of course, the editor doesn't have the script to look at and discover that it's the work of genius that the children's department has been waiting for!

Make a short summary of your work: an outline of the plot showing the involvement of the main characters, giving details of the setting, plus an estimation of the length of the script, if your work is a novel; an outline of the subject matter covered, with details of what is proposed for each chapter or section, plus an estimate of length, and details of your qualifications to write such a book, if it's non-fiction.

Send a copy of the synopsis, plus (if you can manage it) a copy of two chapters, to the publisher of your choice, asking in your covering letter if it would be interested in seeing the complete text. Then, if the reply is favorable, you can submit all the material.

WHAT HAPPENS NEXT

First, you need to be very patient. It takes time, as a rule, to hear from a publisher. It is highly likely that your work will be rejected, by someone, somewhere. You will feel hurt! This is only natural, but it is an occupational hazard in the life of a would-be writer. Even the greatest authors have experienced rejections, so you are in good company.

Try offering your work elsewhere – but if you keep getting rejections, be brave enough to take stock. You may have to decide that trying to become a writer isn't for you.

PROOFREADERS' MARKS

Instructions to printer	Textual mark	Marginal mark	Instructions to printer	Textual mark	Marginal mark
Set in or change to italics	typeface groups	(ital)	Transpose characters or word	groups typeface	(tr)
Set in or change to capitals	typeface groups	(cap)	Transpose characters (2)	tpyeface groups	(tr)
Set in or change to small capitals	typeface groups	(sc)	Transpose lines	The dimensions of / are called set points	(tr)
Capitals for initials small caps rest of word	typeface groups	(cap+sc)	Transpose lines (2)	The dimensions of / are called set points.	(tr)
Set in or change to bold type	typeface groups	(bf)	Center type	typeface groups	(center)
Set in or change to bold italic type	typeface groups	(bf+ital)	Indent 1 em	typeface groups	(indent 1em)
Change capitals to lower case	typeFACE groups	(lc)	Delete indent	typeface groups	(flush left)
Change small capitals to lower case	typeFACE groups	(lc)	Set line justified	typeface groups	(justify)
Change italic to roman	typeface groups	(rom)	Set column justified		(justify col)
Invert type	typeface groups	ʠ	Move matter to right	typeface groups	
Insert ligature	fi/msetter	(fi)	Move matter to left	typeface groups	
Substitute separate letters for ligature	fi/msetter	fi	Take over to next line	typeface groups	(break)
Insert period	typeface groups⊙	⌃○	Take back to previous line	typeface groups	(move up)
Insert colon	typeface groups:	⌃:	Raise matter	typeface groups	
Insert semi-colon	typeface groups;	⌃;	Lower matter	typeface groups	
Insert comma	typeface groups,	⌃,	Correct vertical alignment	typeface groups	‖
Insert quotation marks	typeface groups	⌃ ʻ/ʼ	Correct horizontal alignment	typeface groups	(align)
Insert double quotation marks	typeface groups	⌃ ʻʻ/ʼʼ	Close up space	type face groups	⌒
Substitute character in superior position	typeface groups	(sup)	Insert space between words	typeface groups	#
Substitute character in inferior position	typeface groups	(sub)	Reduce space between words	typeface groups	(reduce #)
Insert apostrophe	typeface groups	⌃ ʼ	Reduce or insert space between letters	typeface groups	#
Insert ellipsis	typeface groups ...	⌃ ○○○	Make space appear equal	typeface groups	(equal #)
Insert leader dots	... typeface groups	⌃ ○○○	Close up to normal line spacing	typeface groups	
Substitute or insert hyphen	typeface groups	⌃ =	Insert space between paragraphs	are called set points. The dimension of	(#)
Insert rule	typeface groups	(2pt rule)	Leave unchanged	typeface groups	(stet)
Insert virgule	typeface groups	⌃ /	Insert new matter	groups	λ typeface
Start new paragraph	are called set points. The dimension of	⌃ ¶	Delete	typeface groups	℮
No fresh paragraph, run on	are called set points. The dimension of	(no ¶)	Delete and close up	typeface groups	℮

IF YOUR WORK IS ACCEPTED

Before an editor goes so far as to commit himself or herself to a contract, he or she may ask for considerable revision to the script. These revisions should be explained to you – just what is wanted and why. If you can carry them out successfully, you will have produced a more salable manuscript, demonstrated your flexibility as a writer – and learned useful lessons for the future! When revisions are required and again when your book is set and you are sent galley proofs to correct, it is wise to learn and use the recognized standard proofreader's marks. This will save time for both your editor and the printer – and consequently it will save money in revision costs. *Don't* use the galley or page proof stage as an opportunity to do a major rewrite – but when any correction *is* necessary – either because of a fault in the setting or to improve or update your text – use the appropriate mark.

The next stage will be an offer – you'll get a letter suggesting certain terms on which the publisher would be prepared to accept your work. This will probably be an offer of an advance payment against specified royalties for home and overseas publication. The advance represents an amount that the publisher thinks will be made either in the first year of the book's life or on the sale of the first edition. It can be paid in several parts – half on signature of the contract and half on publication; alternatively, a third on signature of the contract, a third on signing up a necessary co-edition and a third on publication are options frequently offered. All the sales of the book will eventually be recorded and you will get a copy. YOU WILL NOT RECEIVE ANY ROYALTY PAYMENTS UNTIL YOUR ADVANCE HAS BEEN PAID OFF!

Some kinds of work are bought outright; for example, miscellanies of poetry, games and stories are frequently compiled on a flat fee basis; or, if a short story seems right for a collection, the publisher may want the right to reproduce it only in that collection and payment would be suggested accordingly.

A CONTRACT

If you accept the offer that is made to you, then, and only then, will you get a contract! This is a long legal document, setting out rights and duties on the part of both author and publisher. If you go through a contract you will find that the publisher undertakes to produce your book and to pay certain sums of money both in respect of the original edition and in respect of other "rights" if and when sold. That's to say, if paperback or foreign language rights or the right to manufacture bars of soap or bed linen bearing representations of your characters are sold, the publisher will pay you a stated percentage of money received. The publisher will undertake to try to sell such rights (where appropriate) and will take up the cudgels on your behalf if, say, it's necessary to go to court to protect your copyright.

You will undertake to provide a complete typescript by a given date, which is free from libel or blasphemy or various other disasters. You will correct proofs, and possibly supply additional material if required (for example, information about where exactly highly technical photographs needed for illustration purposes might be found).

- *LOOK OUT* for an option clause. Some firms include them, some don't. If your contract has one, it will commit you to showing your next work to the same publisher. It's usually included to protect the publisher's investment in you – if you're going to be successful, the firm that took you on when you were unknown wants to be around when it happens!
- *LOOK OUT* for details of what happens if the firm stops trading or if your book goes

out of print. The contract should tell you exactly what will happen to your work. If it doesn't, inquire and insist that such terms are written into the contract.

If you're in any doubt about your contract – ask. Your editor should be happy to explain anything that puzzles you. Individual clauses in a contract can be rewritten, so if you particularly want to sell translation rights in Swedish or Mandarin yourself, or you don't feel competent to provide an index, this is the moment to deal with it. Societies and organizations which give legal advice are listed in the *Appendix,* page 138.

AFTER YOU'VE SIGNED YOUR CONTRACT

It takes time to produce a book! You'll find that your publisher may be considering bringing out your work six months, a year or even longer in the future. This takes into account all the various procedures involved – editing and copy-editing, maybe organizing co-editions overseas, guiding illustrations, designing the book, getting the type set, proofreading, indexing, printing, binding, delivering to warehouses – and then publicizing, taking orders, making up and despatching orders from the warehouse, and giving booksellers time to receive and display copies for the publication day.

There may also be a particular reason why your book has been timed to come out at a certain period of the year. Publishers usually time their lists for the spring and fall. Fall allows books to be published in time for Christmas, which is traditionally a good time for buying and selling books. Spring is a good time for sales to schools and is also the season for major conferences and exhibitions – the London Book Fair, the American Booksellers Association meeting, the American Library Association meeting, and the Bologna Children's Book Fair (at which publishers buy rights in books originating overseas – and sell rights in their own titles). The attention of the book trade is firmly fixed on new books in the spring. And, of course, there are all those people who got gift certificates for Christmas!

A WORD (OR SEVERAL) OF WARNING

Booksellers are not obliged to take a book if they don't want to! They buy from publishers what they think they can sell. This may mean that your local bookstore doesn't have copies of your book on publication day, even though the bookseller should have been told about it.

Don't feel disappointed. In fact, it's a good idea to plan to do something very absorbing, and unconnected with books, on publication day. Then you won't feel let down if nothing much happens. Don't expect rave reviews in vast quantities. Your publisher ought to send you copies of notices, but you will probably find that they are fewer and shorter than you had imagined. Some may be critical – and you have to learn to live with that. If you offer work for public consumption, the public may tell you that it doesn't like it. This is a risk you run in trying to get published.

Don't expect to make your fortune overnight! You won't. Don't forget that for the very small handful of authors who do make a living out of writing, there are many thousands of people who don't – but it doesn't prevent them from enjoying a career as a writer in addition to their other jobs.

For most writers, such eventualities are far ahead in the future. The important thing is the manuscript you're writing, or have just completed. Be sensible! Do your research, so you can be reasonably sure you're sending it to the right firm, write a short, straightforward letter, put in your stamped, addressed envelope, wrap up your package carefully and head to the post office.

GOOD LUCK!

Appendix

USEFUL BOOKS AND PERIODICALS

ARTIST'S MARKET. *Writer's Digest.* Published annually. Lists buyers of all types of graphic art, including illustrations; includes names and addresses, pay rates and sales tips.

BEST IN CHILDREN'S BOOKS: THE UNIVERSITY OF CHICAGO GUIDE TO CHILDREN'S LITERATURE 1979-84, *edited by Zena Sutherland. University of Chicago Press (1985).* Earlier editions covered 1966-72 and 1973-1978. Selected reviews evaluated byteachers and librarians.

CHILDREN'S BOOKS IN PRINT. *R.R. Bowker.* Published annually. A guide to all American children's books in print.

THE CHILDREN'S PICTURE BOOK *by Ellen Roberts. Writer's Digest (1981).* Covers all aspects of preparing and selling a book.

ILLUSTRATION & DRAWING: STYLES & TECHNIQUES *by Terry Presnall. North Light (1987).* Covers dozens of illustration and drawing techniques in a variety of media.

NONFICTION FOR CHILDREN *by Ellen Roberts. Writer's Digest (1986).* Comprehensive guide to writing children's nonfiction books.

PHOTOGRAPHING YOUR ARTWORK *by Russell Hart. North Light. (1987).* Guide to making slides of artwork for the nonphotographer.

WRITER'S MARKET. *Writer's Digest.* Published annually. Lists buyers of freelance material, including book publishers.

ORGANIZATIONS

THE AUTHORS LEAGUE OF AMERICA, INC. *234 W. 44th St, New York, NY 10036:* for advice for all authors. Also has sample contracts.

CHILDREN'S BOOK COUNCIL *67 Irving Pl, New York, NY 10003:* deals with both authors and illustrators of children's books.

GRAPHIC ARTISTS GUILD *30 E. 20th st, Room 405, New York, Ny 10003:* for assistance for graphic designers and illustrators in all areas.

JOINT ETHICS COMMITTEE *P.O. Box 179, Grand Central Station, New York, NY 10017:* sponsored jointly by the Art Directors Club of New York, the American society of Magazine Photographers, the Graphic Artists Guild, the Society of Illustrators, and the Society of Photographers and Artists Representatives. Has successfully mediated or arbitrated disputes between graphic artists and clients for 35 years.

POETS & WRITERS *201 W. 54th St, New York, NY 10019:* for information for all authors.

THE SOCIETY OF CHILDREN'S BOOK WRITERS *Box 296, Mar Vista Station, Los Angeles, CA 90066:* deals with both authors and illustrators.

SOCIETY OF ILLUSTRATORS *128 E. 63rd St, New York, NY 10021:* for information for illustrators.

VOLUNTEER LAWYERS FOR THE ARTS *36 W. 44th St, New York, NY 10036:* for free legal services for those meeting income requirements. Referrals to similar organizations in other cities.

Bibliography and Index of Books

Adams, Richard. *Watership Down.* Macmillan, 1974. **Pp10, 53.**.

Ahlberg, Janet and Allan. *Each Peach Pear Plum.* Viking Penguin, 1979. **Pp60, 61.**

The Jolly Postman or Other People's Letters. Little, Brown, 1986. **P115.**

Yum Yum. Viking Kestrel, 1984 (UK). **P119.**

Aiken, Joan. *The Cuckoo Tree.* Jonathan Cape, 1971 (UK). **P26.**

Alcott, Louisa M. *Little Women.* Various edns. First published 1869. **Pp41-42.**

Awdry, Reverand. *Thomas the Tank Engine.* Various

edns. First published 1948. **Pp30, 122.**

Baker, Alan. *Benjamin's Portrait*. Lothrop, Lee & Shepard, 1987. **P65.**
Baum, Louis. *After Dark*. Andersen Press. 1984, (UK). **P47.**
  One More Time. William Morrow, 1986. **Pp48, 50.**
  I Want to See the Moon. Bodley Head, 1984, (UK). **P48.**
Bawden, Nina. *The Peppermint Pig*. Harper & Row Junior Books, 1975. **P33.**
Baylis, Jean and Doreen Smith. *Whose Footprints?* Blackie, 1986, (UK). **P58.**
Berridge, Celia. *Forget-me-not*. Viking Kestrel, (UK). **P67.**
Boston, Lucy. *The Children of Green Knowe*. HBJ, 1977. **P37.**
Bradley, John. Ray Marshall. *The Car*. Viking Penguin, 1984. **Pp109, 119.**
Braithwaite, Althea. *Hippos at Home*. Orchard Books, 1987, (UK). **P105.**
Briggs, Raymond. *Fairy Tale Treasury*. Dell, 1986. **P59.**
  Fungus the Bogeyman. Random House, 1979. **P118.**
  Mother Goose Treasury. Putnam, 1966. **P61.**
  The Snowman. Random House, 1986. **P61.**
  When the Wind Blows. Schocken Books, 1982. **P50.**
Browne, Anthony, *Gorilla*. Alfred A Knopf, 1985. **P48.**
Bruna, Dick. *I Can Count*. Price, Stern, Sloan, 1984. **P57.**
Brunhoff, Jean de. *Story of Babar*. Random House, 1937. **P31.**
Burnett, Frances Hodgson. *A Little Princess*. Various edns. First published 1905. **Pp17, 53.**
  Little Lord Fauntleroy. Various edns. First published 1865. **P16.**
  The Secret Garden. Various edns. First published 1911. **Pp17, 42-43.**

Campbell, Rod. *Buster's Bedtime*. Peter Bedrick Books. **P120.**
  My Favorite Things. Blackie, 1985, (UK). **Pp114.**
  Pocket Wheels Big and Strong. Blackie, 1985, (UK). **Pp116, 118-119.**
Carle, Eric. *The Very Hungry Caterpillar*. Putnam, 1981. **Pp119, 120.**
Carroll, Lewis. *Alice's Adventures in Wonderland*. Various edns. First published 1865. **Pp10, 19.**
  Sylvie and Bruno. Various edns. First published 1889. **P24.**
Chell, Mary. *Edwin's Adventures*. A & C Black, 1979, (UK). **P57.**
Colwell, Eileen. *More Stories to Tell*. Penguin, 1979, (UK). **P12.**
Crompton, Richmal. "William" series. Published Macmillan Children's Books (UK). **P16.**
Crowther, Robert. *Amazing Hide-and-Seek* books.

Viking Penguin. **P117.**

Dickens, Charles. *Sketches by Boz*. Various edns. First pub 1836. **P69.**
Disney, Walt (ed). *Cinderella*. Windmill Books, 1982. **Pp20-21.**
Dupasquier, Philippe. *Our House on the Hill*. Andersen Press, 1987, (UK). **P61.**

Edwards, Dorothy. *My Naughty Little Sister*. Prentice-Hall, 1981. **Pp16, 70.**
Eichenberg, Fritz. *Ape in a Cape*. HPJ, 1973. **P57.**
Evans, C.S. *Cinderella*. Heinemann, 1919, (UK). **Pp11, 20-21.**

Farjeon, Eleanor. "Elsie Piddock Skips in Her Sleep" from *A Storyteller's Choice*. Eileen Colwell (ed). Bodley Head, (UK). **P13.**

Garfield, Leon. *The Strange Affair of Adelaide Harris*. Longman, 1971, (UK). **P28.**
Garland, Sarah. *Having a Picnic*. Atlantic Monthly Press, 1985. **P60.**
Garner, Alan. *Red Shift*. Ballantine, 1981. **P30.**
  The Stone Book (part of the "Stone Book Quartet") Philomel, 1978. **Pp35-36, 37.**
Goodall, John. *Paddy's Evening Out*. Macmillan, 1973. **Pp58, 59.**
Gordon, Ruth. *Making Pencils*. Franklin Watts, 1986, (UK). **P111.**
  Making a Teaset. Franklin Watts, 1986, (UK). **P113.**
Grahame, Kenneth. *The Wind in the Willows*. Various edns. First pub 1908. **Pp10, 17, 45, 46.**
Grimm, the Brothers. *Household Stories*. First pub circa 1812. **Pp10, 20-21.**
Guy, Rosa. *Edith Jackson*. Viking Press, 1978. **P53.**

Haggard, Rider. *King Solomon's Mines*. Various edns. First pub 1885. **P18.**
Harris, Joel Chandler. "Brer Rabbit Stories." Various edns. First published crica 1906. *Jump! The Adventures of Brer Rabbit*. HPJ, 1986. **P38.**
Heide, Florence Parry. *The Shrinking of Treehorn*. Holiday House, 1971. **Pp40-41.**
Hill, Eric. *Where's Spot?* Putnam, 1980. **P56, 57, 119.**
Hoban, Russell. *Bread and Jam for Frances*. Harper & Row Junior Books, 1964. **P67.**
  Birthday for Frances. Harper & Row Junior Books, 1968. **P67.**
Hughes, Ted. *The Iron Man*. Faber, 1968, (UK). **Pp33, 34.**
Boynton, Sandra. *Hippos go Berserk*. Little, Brown, 1986. **P57.**

Jackson, Steve and Ian Livingstone. *Warlock of Firetop Mountain*. Dell, 1983. **P121.**
Jansson, Tove. *Finn Family Moomintroll*. Various edns.

First published 1948. **P27.**
Keats, Ezra Jack. *The Snowy Day.* Viking Penguin, 1962. **P47.**
Keeping, Charles. *Joseph's Yard.* Merrimack, 1986. **Pp90, 91.**
Kightley, Rosalinda. *The Little Red Car.* Walker Books, 1984, (UK). **P57.**
Klein, N. *Girls Can Be Anything.* EP Dutton, 1975. **P52.**

Krementz, Jill. *How it Feels When Parents Divorce.* Alfred A Knopf, 1984. **P50.**

Le Guin, Ursula. *The Wizard of Earthsea.* Hougton Mifflin, 1968. **P33.**
Lewis, C.S. *The Lion, the Witch and the Wardrobe.* Macmillan, 1968, **P51.**
Lurie, Alison. *Clever Gretchen & Other Forgotten Folktales.* Harper & Row Junior Books, 1980. **P52.**

Macdonald, George. *The Princess and the Goblin.* Airmont, 1967. **P29.**
McHargue, Georgess. *Private Zoo.* Viking Press, 1975. **P67.**
Meggendorfer, Lothar. *The Dolls House.* First published 1888; republished, Viking Penguin, 1979. **Pp116-117.**
International Circus. First published 1888. Republished, Viking Penguin, 1980. **P117.**
Miller, Johnathan and David Pelham. *The Human Body.* Viking Penguin, 1983. **P109.**
The Facts of Life. Viking Penguin, 1984. **P119.**
Milne, A.A. *Winnie-the-Pooh.* Various edns. First published 1926. **Pp10, 17.**
Minarik, Else Holmelund. *Little Bear.* Harper & Row Junior Books, 1978. **P67.**

Needle, Jan. *The Wild Wood.* André Deutsch, 1981, (UK). **P45.**
Newton, Suzanne. *I Will Call it Georgie's Blues.* Viking Penguin, 1983. **P31.**
Nesbit, E. *The Phoenix and the Carpet.* Various edns. First published 1904. **P46.**
Nystrom, C. *Mike's Lonely Summer.* Lion Books, 1986. **P50.**

O'Brien, Robert. *Z for Zachariah.* Macmillan, 1975. **P51.**
Oram, Hiawyn. *Angry Arthur.* HBJ, 1982. **P67.**
Oxenbury, Helen. *Helping.* Methuen, 1982, (UK). **P104.**

Parish, Peggy. *Amelia Bedelia.* Harper & Row Junior Books, 1963. **P16.**
Pearce, Philippa. *Minnow on the Say.* Oxford University Press, 1955, (UK). **Pp36, 37.**
Tom's Midnight Garden. Harper & Row Junior Books, 1984. **Pp35, 51.**
Perrault and Gustave Doré. *Fairy Tales.* Various edns. First published 1697. **Pp12, 20-21.**
Pienkowski, Jan. *The Haunted House.* E P Dutton, 1979.

Pp118, 119.
Potter, Beatrix. *The Tailor of Gloucester.* Various edns. First published Frederick Warne and Co, 1902. **P38.**
The Tale of Peter Rabbit. Various edns. First published Frederick Warne and Co, 1900. **Pp33, 38, 39.**
Ransome, Arthur. *We Didn't Mean to Go to Sea.* Various edns. First published 1937. **P42.**
Swallows and Amazons. Various edns. First published 1932. **P42.**
Razzi, Jim. *Zartax! The Invincible Transrobot.* Scholastic, 1985. **P120.**
Roberts, David. *The Superbook of Ships.* Grisewood and Dempsey, 1980, (UK). **P111.**
Ross, Tony. *Stone Soup.* Dial Books for Young Readers, 1987. **P91.**

Seuss Dr. *The Butter Battle Book.* Random House, 1984. **P51.**
Spears, Patricia L. *Angelina.* Eakin Press, 1984. **P16.**
Steig, William. *Abel's Island.* Farrar, Straus & Giroux, 1976. **P39.**
Dominic Farrar, Straus & Giroux, 1972. **P38.**
Stevenson, Robert Louis. *Treasure Island.* Various edns. First published 1883. **Pp18, 33.**
Storr, Catherine. *The Castle Boy.* Faber, 1983, (UK). **P19.**
The Chinese Egg. Faber & Faber, 1982. **P24.**
Marianne amd Mark. Gambit, 1958. **P43.**
Rufus. Gambit, 1969. **P18.**
Sucharov. *Toby's Day.* Red Balloon Books, 1979, UK. **P120.**
Sutton, Eve. *My Cat Likes to Hide in Boxes.* State Mutual Book & Periodical Service, 1985. **P59.**
Swindells, Robert. *Brother in the Land.* Holiday House, 1985. **P51.**

Tatchell, Judy and Dilys Wells, *You and Your Food.* Usborne, 1985, (UK). **P113.**
Tolkien, J.R.R. *The Hobbit.* Various edns. First published 1937. **Pp10, 12, 13, 46.**

Varley, Susan. *Badger's Parting Gifts.* Lothrop, Lee & Shepard Books, 1984. **P50.**
Vipont, Elfrida. *The Elephant and the Bad Baby.* Putnam, 1986. **Pp58, 59.**
Voigt, Cynthia. *Come a Stranger.* Macmillan, 1986. **P53.**
Dicey's Song. Macmillan, 1982. **P53.**
Homecoming. Macmillan, 1981. **P53.**
The Runner. Macmillan, 1985. **P53.**
A Solitary Blue. Macmillan, 1983. **P53.**

Waters, Gaby. *Science Tricks and Magic.* Usborne, 1985, (UK). **P103.**
Wildsmith, Brian. *Brian Wildsmith's ABC.* Franklin Watts, 1963. **P57.**
Wilhelm, H. *I'll Always Love You.* Crown, 1985. **P50.**

Williams, Garth. *The Rabbits' Wedding.* Harper & Row Junior Books, 1958. **P47.**
Williams, Jay. *The Practical Princess.* Chatto, 1979. Parents Magazine Press, 1978, (UK). **P52.**
Williams, Vera. *A Chair for my Mother.* Greenwillow Books, 1982. **P48.**

Music, Music for Everyone. Greenwillow Books, 1984. **P48.**
Something Special for Me. Greenwillow Books, 1983. **P48.**

Yeoman, John. *The Bear's Water Picnic.* Macmillan. **P91.**

Index

Acknowledgements

Every effort has been made to obtain copyright clearance for the illustrations in this book and we do apologize if any omissions have been made.

Quarto would like to thank the following for their help with this publication (abbreviations used — t: top; l: left; b:bottom; c: centre; f:far; m:middle):

p.9 *bl* Natural History Photographic Agency **p.10** *bl* from *Cinderella* illustrated by Arthur Rackham, published by William Heinemann Ltd **p.10** *br* from *Illustrating Children's Books*, illustration by George Cruikshank. Copyright © 1963 Watson-Guptill **p.12** from *The Hobbit* illustrated by the author J.R.R. Tolkien, published by Unwin & Hyman Ltd. © copyright George Allen & Unwin Ltd, 1978. US © copyright Houghton Mifflin Company **p.13** from *More Stories to Tell* illustrated by Caroline Sharpe, published by Penguin Books Ltd. Collection copyright © Eileen Colwell 1979. Illustration copyright © Caroline Sharpe 1979 **p.15** Zefa Picture Library **p.17** *l* from *The Wind in the Willows* line illustration by E.H. Shepard, published by Methuen's Children's Books Ltd. Copyright under the Berne Convention, reproduced by permission of Curtis Brown, London. US © copyright Charles Scribner's Sons, New York **p.17** *r* from *Winnie-the-Pooh* line illustration by E.H. Shepard, published by Methuen's Children's Books Ltd. Copyright under the Berne Convention, reproduced by permission of Curtis Brown, London. US © copyright E.P. Dutton, New York **p.20-21** text excerpt from *Cinderella* by C.S. Evans; published by William Heinemann Ltd, 1919 **p.20-21** text excerpt

Disney, Walt. (Ed) *Cinderella*; published by Collins, 1985 **p.24** from *Sylvie and Bruno* by Lewis Carroll, illustrated by Harry Furniss, published by MacMillan and Co, 1889 **p.26** text excerpt from *The Cuckoo Tree* by Joan Aiken, copyright © 1971 by Joan Aiken; reprinted by permission of Doubleday, a division of Bantam, Doubleday, Dell Publishing Group Inc, New York and Jonathan Cape Ltd, London **p.27** text excerpt from *Finn Family Moomintroll* by Tove Jansson; published by A & C Black (Publishers) Ltd **p.29** text excerpt from *The Princess and the Goblin* by George Macdonald; published by Penguin, 1970 **p.28** text excerpt from *The Strange Affair of Adelaide Harris* by Leon Garfield (Puffin Books, 1974), copyright © Leon Garfield, 1971 **p.35** text excerpt from *Tom's Midnight Garden* by Philippa Pearce (1958) illustrated by Susan Einzig; published by Oxford University Press, 1958 **p.36, 37** text excerpt from *The Stone Book* by Alan Garner (William Collins and Sons, 1976) copyright © Alan Garner **p.38** *bl* from *Jump! The Adventures of Brer Rabbit* published by Methuen's Children's Books Ltd. Copyright © 1986 Van Dyke Parks and Malcolm Jones. Illustration Copyright © 1986 Pennyroyal Press Inc. Harcourt Brace Jovanovich (US) **p.38** *br* from *The Tale of Peter Rabbit* by Beatrix Potter, published by Penguin Books Ltd. Text and original illustrations copyright Frederick Warne & Co, 1902. Copyright under the Berne Convention **p.38** text excerpt from *Dominic* by William Steig Copyright © 1972 reprinted by permission of Farrar, Straus and Giroux Inc **p.39** text excerpt from *The Tale of Peter Rabbit* by Beatrix Potter (Frederick Warne & Co, 1905) copyright © Frederick Warne and Co 1905 **p.39** text excerpt from